To John,
thank you for
being such a good
friend — and no
complaining when
Choryl Johles

Love
Barbara
10·31·90

BEATING
THE MARRIAGE
ODDS

BEATING
THE MARRIAGE
 ## ODDS

*When You
Are Smart,
Single, and
Over Thirty-five*

BARBARA LOVENHEIM

WILLIAM MORROW AND COMPANY, INC.
NEW YORK

Recognizing the importance of preserving what has been written, it is
the policy of William Morrow and Company, Inc., and its imprints and
affiliates to have the books it publishes printed on acid-free paper, and
we exert our best efforts to that end.

Library of Congress Cataloging-in-Publication Data

Lovenheim, Barbara.
  Beating the marriage odds : when you are smart, single, and over
thirty-five / Barbara Lovenheim.
      p. cm.
  Includes bibliographical references.
  ISBN 0-688-08426-5
  1. Mate selection—United States.   2. Marriage—United States.
3. Single women—United States.   I. Title.
HQ801.L657   1990
646.7′7—dc20   90-37647
                                                                            CIP

Printed in the United States of America

First Edition

1 2 3 4 5 6 7 8 9 10

BOOK DESIGN BY RUTH KOIBERT

CONTENTS

Contents

Contents

PROLOGUE

The Quest for the Holy Grail

Several years ago I was sleeping soundly on a Saturday morning when the telephone rang and woke me. When I answered, I heard the hysterical voice of a good friend at the other end:

"Did you read *The New York Times*?" she shrieked. "We're all doomed."

"Doomed?" I said still half asleep and beginning to go over all the dire possibilities in my mind: Were we at war? Did Iran drop a bomb on Israel? Was the president shot? Did fail-safe fail?

"We can't get married," she continued. "It's in the paper. We're too old."

"Too old?" I said, still not quite alert. "Diane, are you crazy?"

My friend, an extremely attractive surgeon in her

late thirties, is usually poised and self-possessed. But her voice rang with tension and anxiety as she went on to describe the article in *The Times*, a devastating study about the marital prospects for single career women that soon rocked the country.

The coauthors of the report, Neil G. Bennett, a sociologist at Yale University, and David E. Bloom, an economist then at Harvard, had set out to investigate why marriage rates in America had fallen dramatically in the past decades. In the course of their research they came out with the grim prophecy that once a single college-educated woman reached thirty-five, her chances of marrying were 5 percent; when she reached forty, her chances of marrying dropped to 1.3 percent.

The two researchers explained that the findings were caused by women's new career ambitions and men's preference for women who are young and not as accomplished. "By the time [these women] want to marry, there are fewer available men to choose from," Dr. Bennett told *The Times*. "Those available are either not the kind of men the women want to marry, or the men prefer women who are younger, not as highly educated or not as successful."[1]

The study soon became fodder for major newspapers and magazines, which highlighted the fact that women who deferred marriage to pursue a career would be educating themselves out of the marriage market. *Newsweek* ran a popular cover story and set up the snappy analogy that a single woman in her forties had a better chance of being killed by a terrorist than marrying. *People* predicted that a spinster boom was on the horizon; even the weighty *Wall Street Journal* explored the study's implications in a front-page column.[2]

As media coverage on the report mounted, it triggered anxiety and panic in women of all ages and marital states. Young women starting out in career paths wondered if they would be able to marry in their thirties. Divorced mothers wondered how they could compete for husbands if single women with no dependents and good jobs were destined to have a tough time.

Why did this report set off such profound reactions in women, many of whom had been beating the odds in their careers? My friend Diane, for example, started out as a home economist. In her late twenties she enrolled in a difficult premed course of studies and mastered physics, chemistry, and math. At thirty she entered medical school. Then she managed to get a residency in a top New York City hospital—and she is currently one of the few female orthopedic surgeons in the country. Her chances of succeeding in her career were certainly less than 5 percent and probably less than 1.3 percent. Yet she was clearly unnerved by the Bennett/Bloom report.

I am no exception to the rule. I've managed to "beat the odds" in my careers as a college professor and journalist. Yet I, too, was stunned and upset by these new findings. After a lot of soul-searching I finally concluded that the report's impact had less to do with its projections than with its implications. It seemed to function as a caustic and definitive rebuttal of feminist goals, a terse warning that women who succeeded in a man's world would no longer be loved—or lovable. If we competed with men—and outpaced them—in business and politics, we would no longer have the *choice* to marry and raise children because men's prevalent bias for younger and less competent females would do us in.

In short it resurrected deep-rooted anxieties about the nature of womanhood that Betty Friedan, the grande dame of feminism, has addressed in her most recent book, *The Second Stage*. She admits that the women's movement was short-sighted when it devalued family life. Women have a basic—and legitimate —need to fulfill their emotional desires and validate their femininity through nurturing relationships with men and children.[3]

Most of us would happily agree with Ms. Friedan's revised views. What she does not address in her passionate analysis of the challenges facing women today is exactly *how* women are going to integrate their need to work and love if so many men seem bent on dismissing career women as sexual partners or mothers.

We seem to have come full circle: What is distressing many women today is not so much the possibility that we won't develop fulfilling careers, it's the gnawing fear that success and age are going to undermine our sexual identities and eliminate our ability to find love—or receive it.

Even though the Bennett/Bloom report has now been seriously challenged—as I'll show later—and the two researchers no longer stand by their projections, the self-doubts and anxieties it brought to the fore have been simmering for many years.

The issue is not simply whether women can—and should—have economic and political parity with men. The question is, At what cost?

Are personal relationships still dependent upon the traditional male and female polarities that imprisoned women in the past?

Are youth and beauty still more prized by men in our society than experience and sagacity?

If we compete successfully with men in business, will they still want to marry us?

Will they love us?

And what, finally, is the solution?

♦

"The difficulty of finding and maintaining a healthy, enduring relationship with a partner of the opposite sex has become a major life problem for increasing numbers of people today," writes John Welwood, a psychologist and editor of *Challenge of the Heart*, a study of love and intimacy. "Not only have the old ties holding couples together been rapidly dissolving, but the very notions of interdependence between men and women, and even heterosexuality itself, have come under increasing scrutiny, if not downright attack. It is hard even to think clearly about the nature of the problem without falling prey to stereotypes, clichés, myths, and fantasies of all kinds."[4]

Clearly this is not exclusively a woman's issue, but it seems to be affecting women more acutely than men because women are more strapped by competing priorities, demographics, and cultural biases than men.

Nor is this issue of finding male partners any longer the singular domain of women's magazines or popular self-help manuals. Just a few years ago *The New York Times* ran a front-page article describing the plight of career women in Manhattan, who, it said, were all coping with "loneliness" and "despair" because they can't find a man to date or marry.[5] Therapists nowadays routinely report that their practices are disproportionately filled with female patients who come in seeking solutions because they are upset and depressed about their single status.

"It's happening more and more," said Kenneth Druck, a psychologist in San Diego with a large practice of single men and women, in a feature article in the *Los Angeles Times*.

"The unmarried, over-thirty woman is coming in

becauses she thinks something is wrong. She has an underlying sense of failure, a nagging suspicion that perhaps she has missed the boat somewhere. The fact is, she doesn't have a relationship. She's not part of a family."[6]

Other therapists who specialize in the problems of unmarried career women relate similar stories. "I see a lot of women," says Diane Adile Kirschner, a family therapist and codirector of the Institute for Comprehensive Family Therapy, in Spring House, Pennsylvania. "They are lawyers, they are women who are into management-level stuff in corporations, and they are doing quite well. At this point in their life, they could care less about their careers. They don't want to hear about advancing. They are physically attractive and they're not overweight. But they come in and say, 'Look, I need to connect with someone. This is the missing piece in my life.' "

For some women the quest for a meaningful relationship has become akin to a religious crusade: They go on strenuous fasts, move to new cities, spend thousands of dollars exploring their psyches and even find new jobs in male-dominated fields in the hope that finding a man—and marrying him—will heal all their inner wounds and validate their identity as females.

"We pursue relationships the way people used to pursue religion," noted Robin Norwood, the author of the best-selling *Women Who Love Too Much*, in a recent interview. "The irony is that women who don't have a man think they'd be fine if they had one, and vice versa."[7]

◆

As a single career woman in my forties and the former president of a large singles club in Manhattan with a base of professional men and women, I am not immune to these fears or the pressures they have created in women. Many of my single women friends have achieved great professional success, but they go through periods of panic and depression because they can't seem to find a man who appreciates them and is willing to sustain a relationship. Other women I know have simply given up—they rarely date and spend almost all their leisure time in the company of women friends.

When I decided to write this book, I did so because I wanted to see if marrying in midlife was really Mission Impossible for the scores of women who now profess that finding a mate is the chief priority in their lives. In the course of my research I interviewed over seventy-five women in their late thirties, forties, and fifties from a variety of large and medium-size American cities who married later in life.

Many were single career women who married for the first time in their forties; others were working mothers who remarried many years after they were divorced. Some bore children for the first time over thirty-five. I wanted to find out what distinguished them from unmarried women who complain about the difficulties of finding—and maintaining—relationships with men.

Did they develop any strategies that enabled them either to meet men or to be more receptive when suitable men presented themselves?

Did they experience internal changes that triggered their decision—and ability—to marry?

Did they go through extensive therapy?

Were they all exceptionally good-looking?

Did they change their life-styles in order to find a mate?

Did they rescale their expectations and compromise?

Were they simply lucky?

◆

What I discovered was partly discouraging—but ultimately reassuring. Most women over thirty-five do have a difficult time finding mates because unmarried women outnumber unmarried men. But the male shortage is only one factor working against women today—and perhaps not the most important difficulty.

The chief problem is the feeling of inner emptiness and angst that many women are now experiencing, and, as Betty Friedan points out, these feelings are not characteristic of unmarried women only. They are apt to occur in any woman—or man, for that matter—who does not feel centered and depends upon another person to invest her or him with self-worth.

Ms. Friedan, the mother of three children, commented that what drove her to explore the issues that stirred up the women's movement was a "driving need to *feel good* about being a woman, about myself as a woman, to be able to affirm who I really am—*All that I am I will not deny.* Not only in my secret heart of hearts, but in the reality of evolving life, in the world."[8]

Almost all the women I interviewed echoed these sentiments in various ways: Before they were able to find a man who really valued them, they had to come to terms with their own core and value themselves. Self-healing—and validation in the world—are necessary parts of the process, because it is only when you genuinely learn to hold yourself in high regard and take charge of your environment that you can release the psychic energies and strength needed to recognize available men—and be receptive to them when they present themselves.

Women who succeed in marrying do so less by employing artificial strategies, which are almost destined to fail because they are artificial, than by nurturing certain positive attitudes about themselves. The benefit of this process is that even if you do not connect with a man immediately or in the long run, you will develop the capacity to enjoy life on your own and validate your womanhood in the world.

Immanuel Kant, an eighteenth-century German philosopher, said that the real challenge of life was taking the given and raising it to the level of the self-created. Translated into less lofty terms, Kant was saying that you can only begin to make choices when you *understand* the limitations of your environment, your psychological makeup, and your needs.

The choices that women have today with men may indeed be limited and far from ideal—but what choices are ever ideal? The task is to understand the nature of those choices so that you can act as effectively as possible. And the sheer process of acting can alleviate much of the depression that causes women to feel helpless and victimized.

This does not mean that a suitable man will rise up out of the sea when good attitudes develop. I don't subscribe to the view that "readiness" is all—and none of the women I interviewed did either. "Readiness" is only part of the process. The male shortage is real. There are many men who don't want sustaining connections. You have to recognize these very real limitations and be willing to persist—in addition to cultivating a good self-image—if marrying is your goal.

The key issue, after all, is not simply finding a marriageable man: the key issue is knowing who you are and what you want. What works for some women doesn't work for others. Some women I interviewed made accommodations that other women would find repugnant. Others used strategies that many would find offensive or uncomfortable. Some women set up marriage as a priority; others met a man when they decided not to look for a man anymore.

In other words, there are many roads to Rome. But if Rome is your goal, you have to set up an itinerary that will take you to Rome and not Outer Mongolia. Also you have to find a path that will suit you and not your best friend, so that even if you don't make it to Rome, you will enjoy the journey. And you have to decide why you want to go, to see if Rome is really what you're after.

But before you begin your journey, let's look at the realistic choices you do have. As I'll shortly point out, there are many more choices than the infamous Bennett/Bloom study led us to believe. There is, fortunately, good reason for hope.

O N E

Marriage Prophecies:
A New Look

The Bennett/Bloom study set off such a furor about the marriage prospects for single women that other demographers have taken it to task. Shortly after the report was published, Jeanne E. Moorman, a demographer at the United States Bureau of the Census, released a more optimistic paper based on 1980 and 1985 data. Her report projected that college-educated, single, thirty-five-year-old women had a 32 to 41 percent chance of marrying; forty-year-old women had a 17 to 23 percent chance of marrying; and forty-five-year-old women had a 9 to 11 percent chance.[1]

In the past two years two studies have been released describing the marital prospects for divorced women. The first, put together by a team of researchers at the

University of Wisconsin, projects that about 60 percent of women who separate from their husbands in their thirties will rewed, but only a third of the women who separate from their husbands after forty will do so.[2] The second, compiled by researchers at the University of North Carolina, predicts that by the year 2000 almost a third of baby-boom women will be either divorced, single, or widowed. By the time these women reach their sixties, almost half will be unmarried.[3]

Are they accurate?

The Baby Boom Barometer

It is difficult to assess these various studies because they were all developed by competent social scientists using different formulas. But it is now clear that the Bennett/Bloom study was seriously misleading—even the authors have admitted that their projections were too extreme.[4]

Demographers now point out that Bennett and Bloom went awry because they used a formula based on faulty assumptions. They assumed that nearly all women married in their early twenties, partly because this was the norm during the baby boom era (1946–1956) when women were marrying in greater numbers—and at earlier ages—than at any previous time in recent history (see chart A).

When feminism and the sexual revolution developed in the late 1960s, scores of college-educated women began rebelling against the fierce marriage ethic of the postwar period. Instead of marrying early in life, they prepared themselves for careers. First marriage rates (the number of marriages per one

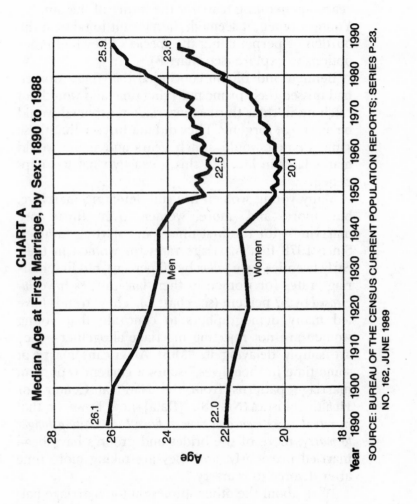

CHART A
Median Age at First Marriage, by Sex: 1890 to 1988

SOURCE: BUREAU OF THE CENSUS CURRENT POPULATION REPORTS; SERIES P-23,
NO. 162, JUNE 1989

thousand single women) fell dramatically and the number of single females over the age of fifteen swelled from 17 million in 1970 to 23 million in 1987—a growth of 35 percent in just seventeen years—generating fears for the future of the family.[5] Young women, it seemed, didn't want to take on the burden of perpetuating the species. They had other options to explore (see chart B).

Bennett and Bloom concluded that these women had missed their prime marrying time and would not catch up in their thirties: marriage postponed would be marriage forgone. They did not foresee that these same women would switch gears and many would marry later in life. But this is exactly what has happened.

Many young women are still deferring marriage, but more and more women over thirty are marrying—for the first time—and starting families. Since 1978 first marriage rates for women in their early twenties have *fallen* by 26 percent, but first marriage rates for women in their late thirties have *increased* by 37 percent (see chart C). These trends have led many demographers to conclude that young women are not rejecting marriage altogether—they are simply delaying it. "Most Americans marry at some time in their lives," states a current report on marriage patterns from the National Center for Health Statistics (NCHS). "[Data] show, however, that *in recent years men and women have been waiting longer to marry,* more of the brides and grooms have been married previously, and they are taking more time after divorce to remarry."[6]

What about the other studies on the marriage patterns of divorced women? One reason the Wisconsin projections may be off base is the fact that the researchers calculated probabilities based on the age at

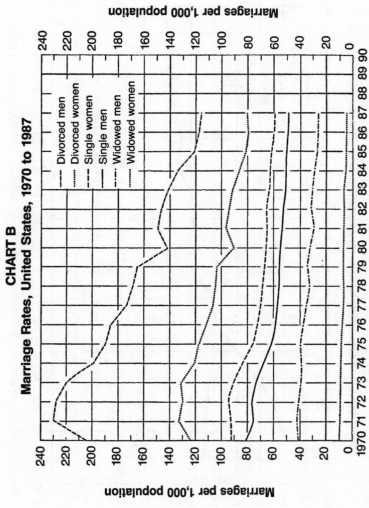

CHART B
Marriage Rates, United States, 1970 to 1987

Marriages per 1,000 population

— — Divorced men
· · · · Divorced women
— — — Single women
— · — Single men
— · · — Widowed men
· · · · · · Widowed women

240 220 200 180 160 140 120 100 80 60 40 20 0

1970 71 72 73 74 75 76 77 78 79 80 81 82 83 84 85 86 87 88 89 90

Marriages per 1,000 population

240 220 200 180 160 140 120 100 80 60 40 20 0

SOURCE: MONTHLY VITAL STATISTICS REPORT, APRIL 3, 1990, NATIONAL CENTER FOR HEALTH STATISTICS

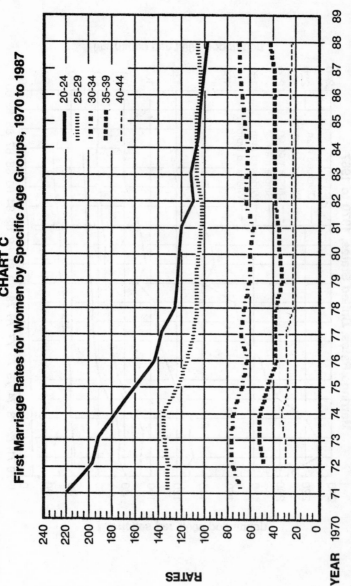

CHART C

First Marriage Rates for Women by Specific Age Groups, 1970 to 1987

SOURCE: DIVISION OF VITAL STATISTICS, MONTHLY REPORTS, 1970 TO 1990, NATIONAL CENTER FOR HEALTH STATISTICS

which a woman separates from her husband—and they did not calculate probabilities for women who were already divorced at that age. Yet we all know that a woman who separates from her husband at forty is simply not in the same boat as a forty-year-old divorced woman who has had time to adapt to single life.

More to the point, none of these reports highlights the fact that even though marriage prospects for older women seem to be dim, more women are marrying —and remarrying—in midlife than ever before, because the pool of divorced adults is expanding so fast. In 1987, for example, an estimated 611,000 American men over thirty-five married, and 453,000 American women over thirty-five also married. Sixty-two thousand of these women were over fifty-five, and 3,500 (of the women over fifty-five) were marrying for the first time.

Indeed more men over the age of thirty-five do marry than women who are their peers, but the majority of these men do not marry much younger women. As I will discuss in chapter 3, the great majority of these men marry women who are only five to eight years younger than they are.

Men don't marry turtles; women don't marry antelopes. They marry each other, even in midlife.

One other reason these various reports are misleading is that they focus exclusively on the marriage prospects for older women and don't take into account the marriage prospects for older men. By omission they fuel the widely held view that almost all divorced men remarry and that their chances are not affected adversely by age.

Is this really true? Are men insulated from the pressures of time that seem to impose stresses on marriage-minded women?

In order to set the matter straight, I asked Barbara

Foley Wilson, a demographer in NCHS who has been tracking marriage patterns for over fifteen years, to calculate marriage probabilities for single men as well as single women.

She developed a set of projections drawing upon the most recent marriage rates available and using a formula common to calculations of life expectancy.[7] According to Mrs. Wilson's calculations (see chart D), *over a third* of single women in their late thirties will eventually marry; *a quarter* of single women in their early forties will marry; *a sixth* of women in their late forties will marry; and almost *a tenth* of women in their early fifties will marry. As chart D also shows, single men are only slightly more likely to marry than single women.

Remarriage rates (the number of marriages per thousand divorced people) show that divorced women, as a group, marry more frequently than either single men or single women, and, not surprisingly, divorced men are the most likely of all to marry. But men as well as women are affected by age. As chart E shows, older men are *less* likely to marry than younger men: A divorced man in his late thirties is 60 percent more likely to marry than a divorced man in his early fifties.

A man's age, however, is not the only factor that influences his marrying prospects. The period of time he spends on his own after his divorce is also critical. Most men who remarry do so quickly after divorce occurs: In 1987, 70 percent who remarried had been divorced five years or less—50 percent remarried within two and a half years of divorce.

Most divorced women who remarry do so relatively quickly as well, but as they age, they tend to spend more time between marriages than men do. As I will discuss in chapter 7, a greater percentage may re-

CHART D
Marriage Probabilities
for Single (Never-Married)
Women and Men

AGE	SINGLE WOMEN	SINGLE MEN
15-19	86%	84%
20-24	84%	83%
25-29	74%	76%
30-34	56%	62%
35-39	38%	46%
40-44	24%	33%
45-49	15%	21%
50-54	9%	14%
55-59	5%	8%
60-64	3%	5%
65 plus	.07%	6%

SOURCE: DIVISION OF VITAL STATISTICS, NATIONAL CENTER FOR
HEALTH STATISTICS, 1987 MARRIAGE RATES

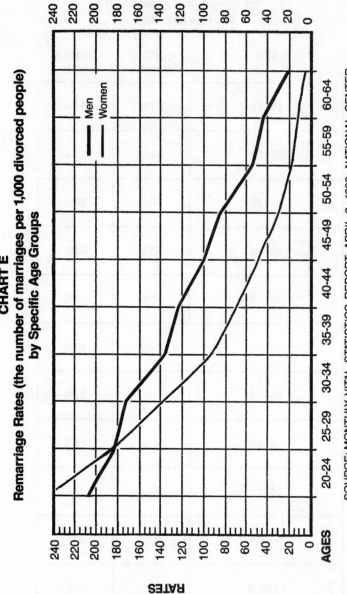

CHART E

Remarriage Rates (the number of marriages per 1,000 divorced people) by Specific Age Groups

RATES

AGES

240 220 200 180 160 140 120 100 80 60 40 20 0

Men
Women

20-24 25-29 30-34 35-39 40-44 45-49 50-54 55-59 60-64

SOURCE: MONTHLY VITAL STATISTICS REPORT, APRIL 3, 1990, NATIONAL CENTER FOR HEALTH STATISTICS

marry years after their divorce occurs than do men who are their counterparts.

And contrary to common wisdom, widowers are *less* likely to remarry than divorced men. NCHS reports that only 19 percent will wed again, primarily because so many men are widowed late in life. A quarter remarry in their second year of widowhood, and after that period of time the likelihood that they will remarry goes down.

The Moral of the Story

Women who are actively looking for marriage partners should keep these statistics in mind. Younger men may be more viable as marriage partners than older men. But if a man is newly divorced or widowed he may marry more readily than a younger man who has been unmarried for many years. And bachelors in midlife are just as likely—or not likely—to marry as men who have been divorced or widowed for many years.

So much for men. What do these statistics reveal about women? For one thing, they show that a woman's marital probabilities really do decline as she ages. That is a fact. The bright side of these statistics is that a large number of woman can—and do—marry at every age. A forty-year-old single woman can find a husband and so can a fifty-two-year-old single woman. A thirty-eight-year-old divorced woman may find a new spouse, and a forty-nine-year-old divorced woman is not at all out of the running.

However, there's an old adage that states, "There are lies, there are damn lies—and then there are statistics." Before you take these statistics too much to heart, you have to realize that statistics describe only the behavior of a group.

What statistics don't reveal is even more important: the personalities of the people in each group and the professions of the people in each group. And, *more important, statistics don't measure intent.* They don't reveal how many people in each group *want* to get married. They reveal only how many people in each group do get married.

We've probably all been out with divorced men who are so comfortable with their life-style as single men that trying to lasso them into marriage is akin to pinning down a bronco. No amount of prodding, pleading, feminine wiles, or threats will cause a man who does not want to marry to change his mind. On the other hand, we've also heard countless stories about die-hard bachelors who suddenly wind up with a wife in midlife, or divorced men who remarry after a fifteen-year stint on their own. Some of the men I interviewed for this book married after having been divorced for ten or even eighteen years. We all know why these men reverse course when the odds seem pitted against *them:* They simply change their minds, and the triggers, as I'll point out in chapter 8, may vary for a number of reasons, from the death of a parent to a sudden confrontation with their own mortality.

Your Real Chances of Marrying May Be Better Than You Think

We tend to overlook that who you are and what you want are critical. One simple reason the marriage odds for single men and single women are so similar—and are so much lower than the marriage odds for divorced men and women—is that there's a hard core of single people who simply don't want to get married. This group includes gay men and lesbians, priests and nuns, and people of both genders who clearly prefer a life of independence.

Consequently, if you really want to figure out your own chances of marrying, you have to realize that your own personality and desire to marry play a significant role. For example, let's suppose you are a single woman in your forties and your statistical odds of marrying are roughly four to one. That means that out of a random group of one hundred single women in their forties, about twenty-five will eventually marry.

But you have to keep in mind that this random group of one hundred women includes a large number of woman who, for the reasons just mentioned, don't want to marry. There may be only fifty women in the group who are comparable to you in personality, appearance, proximity to men, and dating behavior. Within this group of fifty women there may be only thirty who really want to get married. The others may pay lip service to the concept of marriage, but they have many conflicts about it. Therefore if you happen to be one of the women who does want to marry, your chances of eventually finding a spouse may be 50 percent—or even 90 percent. The same dynamics govern women who are divorced—and men as well. Men who *want* to marry are more likely marriage prospects than men who don't want to marry. Their attitude is more important than their age or marital history.

Let's take another example. Nowadays half of all marriages are expected to break up. This doesn't take into account the duration of the marriages and the ages of the spouses. Researchers have shown that people who are older when they marry are less likely to experience a divorce than people who are very young when they marry.[8] In other words, if you marry when you are forty-two, the odds that you will divorce are lower than if you marry when you are twenty-two.

On the other hand, even women who sincerely want to get married have to confront the stern reality that is also highlighted in these statistics: Men really do marry and remarry more frequently and sooner than women. Women who genuinely want to get married have fewer male partners in their sphere as they age, and therefore it may take them more time to find spouses. They usually have to spend more energy locating partners than men; they may have to spend longer periods of time on their own between marriages; and they may also have to work very hard developing the inner resources and self-confidence that will help them navigate in a sea where women outnumber men.

The male shortage is a reality, and *it is not a woman's fault*. It can't be fixed by therapists or plastic surgeons. It can't be fixed by affirmative action. It is not fair. It is not just. It is simply a reality.

How did it happen?

Sex Ratios Run Amok

According to current census data there are 6.5 million unmarried (single, divorced, widowed, and separated) men age thirty-five to fifty-four, and 8.3 million unmarried women age thirty-five to fifty-four. The imbalance is more pronounced as women age because there are so many widows, but the ratio begins work-

ing against women when they pass thirty-five and unmarried women begin to outnumber unmarried men.
At forty, the ratio of unmarried women to unmarried
men becomes 4 to 3; at forty-five the ratio becomes 2
to 1 (see chart F).

Education also upsets the scales: Roughly 1.6 million of these men and 1.6 million women have college
degrees, but women with advanced degrees outnumber men with advanced degrees by a slight margin.
Since men often marry "down"—and women try to
marry "up"—highly educated women are affected the
most severely since they are competing with younger
and less well-educated women for the same men.

The large presence of gay men in the group—who
outnumber gay women by an appreciable margin—
also intensifies the male shortage for women.

What caused the shortage? Even though more boy
babies are born than female babies, male mortality
rates are twice as high as female mortality rates, beginning in infancy: More boy babies die in early childhood than female babies, and during adolescence
more boys than girls are killed in car crashes, wars,
and homicides. Even so, the surplus of females is mi-
nuscule in the early years of life, and it doesn't affect
single women in their twenties because women tend
to marry sooner than men and, when they do, they
tend to marry men who are on the average two years
older than they are.

As a result single men in their twenties *outnumber*
single women, and this ratio continues through the
early thirties, when unmarried men still outnumber
unmarried women by a ratio of about 6 to 5.

But when women reach their mid-thirties, the number of unmarried men and women evens out, partly
because men's rising mortality rates begin to create a
small pool of young widows. And there are about

CHART F

Ratio of Unmarried Men per 100 Unmarried Women: 1988

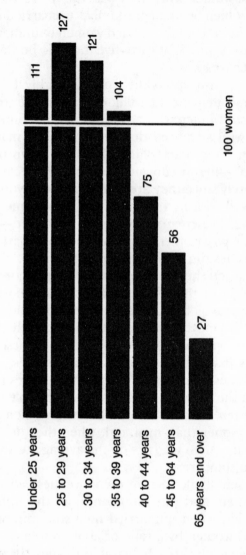

- Under 25 years — 111
- 25 to 29 years — 127
- 30 to 34 years — 121
- 35 to 39 years — 104
- 40 to 44 years — 75
- 45 to 64 years — 56
- 65 years and over — 27

100 women

SOURCE: BUREAU OF THE CENSUS CURRENT POPULATION REPORTS; SERIES P-23, NO. 162, JUNE 1989

600,000 *more* women age forty to forty-four in the entire population than there are men age forty to forty-four.

The real cause of the imbalance, however, is our steep divorce rate and the fact that when men remarry in midlife, they select wives from somewhat younger —and larger—pools of unmarried women. As a result the pool of available older men shrinks more rapidly than the pool of available women who are their peers, and more and more women are competing for fewer and fewer older men.

If divorce were not so prevalent, women in midlife would not have to contend with a male shortage. In England and Wales, for example, where divorced men and women still form a scant 5 percent of the adult population, unmarried men age thirty-five to fifty-four outnumber unmarried women who are their peers.[9] And this is because there are more single (never married) men than single women in Great Britain.

The same situation, incidentally, is true in the United States: Single (never-married) men in their thirties, forties, and fifties outnumber single women who are their peers, but this favorable ratio is offset by the large number of divorced women and widows, who outnumber divorced men and widowers by a wide margin.

Consequently middle-aged women in the United States are caught in the grip of a male shortage that has been set in motion by our steep divorce rate and the prevailing tendency of men to marry younger women. Some demographers point out that this situation is parallel to the early years of the century, when divorce was not common but scores of men and women were widowed prematurely in life.

When men were widowed because their wives died

in childbirth or from the debilitating diseases we have conquered today, they tended to select younger spouses, partly because young women had more energy to take care of their children or to bear more. But widows were often left high and dry because it was harder to find unattached men who had the desire—or money—to take on new families.

According to a life table on marriage patterns prepared by Robert Schoen, a demographer at the University of Illinois, over a quarter of the men born at the turn of the century were widowed—and 40 percent of these men remarried. In contrast over half of the women born at the turn of the century were widowed, but only a scant 14 percent of them managed to remarry.[10]

In short since 1900 there have always been more unmarried women in midlife than unmarried men, and because dating wasn't really an option for many of these women, they didn't expect to marry. They tended to be content raising their own children or living with a married son or daughter and socializing with female friends. As a result they tended to be insulated from the pressures that many women are experiencing today.

Supply and Demand: A New Look

Most of us are familiar with the dynamics of supply and demand, and we know how they operate in the workplace when a lot of skilled workers are chasing a small number of jobs. Similar dynamics operate in the social environment when available women outnumber available men. Men, who are in "demand," tend to behave like employers. Some become cavalier about making commitments or even returning phone calls, they may become overly selective and fussy about women because they have so many choices. Others latch onto the first woman who comes along simply to avoid making choices. Some men focus too soon, some don't focus at all.

Women, who are in "supply," tend to feel victimized and put upon by the small number of potential male partners who seem to be available. They tend to react the way job candidates behave: Some women become aggressive and competitive about finding mates; others devise clever strategies and invest heavily in job counselors—or therapists—to help them out. Still others stop dating because the competition is too tough to handle; they become so devastated after one or two rejections that they lose the ability or incentive to go out and look for a date.

Marcia Guttentag and Paul Secord, social psychologists and the coauthors of a provocative and well-documented book, *Too Many Women? The Sex Ratio Question (1983)*, argue that whenever sex ratios are seriously out of whack, they affect the way in which men and women relate to each other in the initial stages of courtship.[11] The authors also stress that sex ratios *do not* have a significant impact on relationships when real bonding, trust, and loyalty develop and the rewards of a committed union outweigh the dubious pleasures—and real stresses—of severing that union.

"A shortage means that an appreciable number of women will have emotionally disturbing experiences with men," they write. "Moreover, the surplus of women will lead men to value women less, to be less committed to any one woman, and to deemphasize the traditional relationships between men and women and the traditional roles that accompany them. But when the situation is the other way around, when sex ratios are high and there is a shortage of women, men value women more and treat women very differently, though on their own terms."[12]

In patriarchal societies with a "high sex ratio"—an abundance of men and a scarcity of women—men tend to value women as prizes. They compete for women's favors; they marry quickly to secure them; and they set up stiff penalities for wives who don't remain loyal. Since women are in demand, they have the upper hand in the initial stages of courtship. They may become overly fussy and choosy about selecting partners, and they may put their suitors through a stringent series of tests to prove their loyalty and interest.

Courtly love—the tradition that still underlies our current notions of romantic love—developed in the early Middle Ages, when there were few desirable women from noble families and many men sought these women out to improve their status in life. These highborn ladies were idealized in song and poetry, and men competed for their favors by wooing them with gifts and sonnets and tried to prove themselves worthy by performing heroic feats. They often suffered profoundly because these women weren't available. Because a high sex ratio has been the norm in most Western societies, where women married earlier in life than men, the cult of courtly love has persisted throughout the centuries.

We're still conditioned by these norms. Maybe men are no longer writing songs of love for women, except in the sentimental comedies of Rogers and Hart, but we typically expect men to woo us with fancy dinners, flowers, extravagant compliments, and grandiose gestures; men typically boast about their prowess in business or sports to impress us.

But when sex ratios change in patriarchal societies

and there is a low sex ratio—an abundance of females and a scarcity of men—everything shifts. Men tend to devalue women because they are no longer a rarity; they often resist marrying because they have more power—and fewer obligations—when they are free. Promiscuity often flourishes.

Throughout history most civilizations have experienced male shortages that were usually triggered by devastating wars or plagues that tended to wipe out men sooner than women. Many women survived because they were evacuated from infested areas before men. But the economics and value structures of postwar societies vary widely. Even so, two trends set in motion by a shortage of marriageable men usually develop that are interconnected: Women become extremely accommodating to men because there's a scarcity, and they either marry very quickly or find ways of living without men. Because men are typically in charge of the power structure, many tend to become authoritarian or misogynistic in their treatment of women.

In the late Middle Ages, for example, when there was an acute shortage of young men because so many were killed in the Crusades and by the bubonic plague, fathers were hard pressed to find husbands for their daughters. As a result there was a rash of "dowry" inflation, which had to be curbed by legislation. Many noblewomen married "down," making it virtually impossible for lower-class women to find husbands. The age of brides continually dropped as parents tried to marry off their daughters as soon as possible. Many women who didn't want to compete for husbands—or couldn't—set up alternate lifestyles for themselves in a nonreligious female sect known as the Beguines.

During this era the themes of courtly love in literature were replaced by narratives in which marriage was denounced or at least questioned, and misogyny and prostitution flourished. In *The Romance of the Rose*, the most important epic poem of the thirteenth century, the author Jean de Meung writes, "A faithful wife was hardly to be found in the whole of France and the wise man should follow the dictates of nature and seek to perpetuate his kind at every available opportunity."[13]

Throughout Western Europe great wars often decimated significant numbers of marriageable men, leaving young women hard-pressed to find husbands. Even so, few historians have addressed the phenomenon. In our own century, World War II created an unprecedented shortage of men. The Soviet Union was hit hardest. Approximately twenty million Russians died in the course of the war, and most of these victims were men. Some women were able to move up the occupational hierachy because so few men returned, but they suffered on the domestic front. According to Bernice Rosenthal, a professor of Russian history at Fordham University, the postwar male shortage created so much competition to get a husband—and keep him—that women tended to cater to men. Most working wives didn't make demands on their husbands to share household and child-rearing tasks. The term "second shift" was often used to describe the hard lot of women there.[14]

Fortuitously America has been largely insulated from these stresses, since the high number of men migrating to the United States throughout the years has generally offset the number of men killed in war. As a result high sex ratios have prevailed here since colonial days.

Even so, when America entered World War II and over 16 million young men entered military service, college campuses were depleted of male students, and coeds had to scramble for dates. "The hardest hit were those of courting age—especially college girls, who were isolated in an environment that was not at all what it was supposed to be," writes Beth Bailey, a social historian at Barnard College, and the author of *From Front Porch to Back Seat*, a study of courtship patterns in America.[15]

Female students at Northwestern set up a dating service offering to supply cars and expenses for men who would take them to the junior prom. Other coeds lowered their standards and expectations. At Harvard and Radcliffe *The Crimson*, the campus newspaper, reported in December 1945,

> The almost pathetic eagerness of the girl who gets a date is apt to have a dangerous effect on the tender side of the susceptible male. . . . [Once] the Copley, the Ritz, or, in a pinch, the Statler, was the only place to dine. [Now] a snack at Liggetts, or—in the case of a particularly heavy date—supper at Hayes-Bick is gratefully accepted by any girl. . . . Women have lost the initiative. . . . Now rules the strong, silent Harvard man.[16]

When men began returning after the war, euphoria about America's victory was undercut by grim prophecies that one out of every seven women would not find a spouse. "She got a man, but six to eight million women won't. We're short one million bachelors!" announced an article in *Good Housekeeping* in October 1946.[17]

These fears turned out to be partially unfounded, since American losses in World War II were lower than expected—roughly 300,000 men were killed in battle. Even so, the war upset the high sex ratios that had prevailed before 1940, and women felt they were in a precarious situation.

For the first time in American history, there were more women than men. Experts warned young women in dozens of magazine and newspaper articles that a significant portion of women in their age group would never marry because of the sexual imbalance. Women overreacted to the warnings, and the "scarcity" of men became a commonplace justification for all sorts of acts. At the same time, American men were berating American women for being "unfeminine" in contrast with their European sisters (and 90,000 American servicemen had married foreign brides by 1946). Men, being "scarce," were in a strong position in courtship, and many said, flatly and publicly, that they wanted submissive, feminine women. If "femininity" would provide the edge in the race for a husband, many women declared themselves willing to go along.[18]

Women began marrying at younger and younger ages, and the median age at first marriage plummeted to a new and historic low: In 1951, 47 percent of all brides were married before they turned nineteen—a far cry from the early part of the century, when the average age of marriage for women hovered between twenty-one and twenty-two.

Of course the soaring postwar marriage rates that prevailed after 1945 were not simply a response to the fear of a male shortage: Men as well as women craved the stability of family life, and marriage became idealized as a way of insulating everyone from the uncertainty and despair that had characterized America since 1930. But according to Beth Bailey, the fear of a male scarcity continued to haunt women throughout the 1950s and '60s. Many were propelled into early marriages by their mothers who, brought up in the war years and The Great Depression, reminded them that men were hard to come by and that marriage deferred could turn out to be marriage forgone.

Nowadays we are no longer living in the Middle Ages or the aftermath of a world war. Feminism and the sexual revolution have given women new options: Many are no longer dependent upon husbands as their sole means of support, status, or sexual fulfillment. They have more freedom to demand what they want in marriage or dating relationships.

Women lawyers, in short, don't have to marry carpenters or offer bounties to men who will marry them. Nor do they have to settle for a hamburger at McDonald's if they are willing to share the cost of dining at the Four Seasons.

But some trends have developed that are clearly a response to the shortage of middle-aged unmarried men. Many men are hesitant to make a long-term commitment to any one woman, because they don't have to. Many women have taken on the behavior of courtly lovers, experiencing waves of agony and angst as they pine for unavailable men. Other women put themselves through strenuous ordeals and self-improvement tasks to prove themselves worthy and to attract men. A host of current self-help books focus almost exclusively on the prevalence of misogyny: *Men Who Hate Women: The Women Who Love Them; Men Who Can't Love*, and *How to Love a Difficult Man* are just a few recent titles that come to mind.

There's a total absence of books advising men how to woo a difficult woman or how to avoid women who hate men or how to go on stringent diets and redo their psyches in order to make themselves more appealing to women who are demanding, resistant, and self-indulgent.

According to Guttentag and Secord men may not even be conscious that they are a desirable elite. But if they are single for a period of time and realize that it's not hard to find female partners who are accommodating, they unconsciously begin to behave in ways that work against women. One divorced man explained it this way: "There were a lot of women available to me and therefore I found excuses not to play relationships out. For a long time I went through the 'around-the-corner syndrome' that a lot of guys go through: The woman sitting across from you at dinner is wonderful, but the one at the next table is perfect because she doesn't slurp her soup. How can I get into this if there is a party next week? There will always be someone better. Or someone different."

The woman having dinner with this type of man can feel put upon and devalued. She's not slurping her soup and she's even prettier than the woman at the next table. So why does he keep looking at the next woman? His date thinks, Maybe I'm wearing the wrong dress or my hair is falling into my face. Maybe I'm not good enough.

Good enough for what? Good enough to be prized, courted, and valued. Instead of asking, What's wrong with him? she tends to turn the situation inward and say, What's wrong with me? She may linger in bad relationships simply because the prospect of finding another man seems so formidable and she doesn't want to be alone. She may redouble her efforts to satisfy a man—and she may press him for a Saturday night date before he leaves her living room.

He's thinking, It's only Sunday and it's too soon to decide about the weekend. I'm not sure I want to set up a regular pattern just yet. Maybe I'll ask Marilyn instead, or maybe I'll have to prepare a new brief and I won't know until Friday. Besides, I'm taking her out. I'm paying. So I'll call her when I decide.

She's thinking, It's already Sunday night and we've

already slept together. Does he really think I'm into casual sex? I have to lead my life and I want to plan my week. So does it really hurt if I do a bit of gentle coaxing? Besides, it will show him I am really interested.

"[A woman] may have to put up with various behaviors on his part that she finds distressing or obnoxious," say Guttentag and Secord. "She may have to provide outcomes for him that are psychologically costly for her, while he can easily balk at providing outcomes for her if they are costly to him. If, in spite of her efforts, he abandons her for another woman, her feelings of rejection and her resentment are apt to be multiplied by the uneven exchange in which she has given more than he has. She will have a strong sense of having been unfairly treated, which may intensify her feelings of being impotent and powerless. She put forth extra effort and yet was rejected."[19]

Even women in their twenties are not immune to these pressures and feelings. Although they may have numbers on their side, many have been conditioned to marry—and date—"up": Female lawyers may be vying for the same men as their secretaries, or, to paraphrase Connell Cowan and Melvyn Kinder, coauthors of *Smart Women: Foolish Choices*, 80 percent of the women are always chasing 20 percent of the men.[20]

Some women respond to the situation by intensifying their efforts to meet a man—and they go out of their way to please him when they do. "In order to make a man fall in love with you, you must first understand how he perceives his world," advises Tracy Cabot, the author of *How to Make a Man Fall in Love with You*. "Then you can find the key to his heart. . . . Dress in his favorite color. Dress like he does. If he's preppy, you dress preppy. If he's elegant, you be elegant."[21]

Maybe cloning works for slaves, but what if you're

a corporate vice president? Will you be happy with a man who wants a serf?

Other women tend to write men off completely because it's too tough to handle the competition and the attendant feelings of abandonment and anxiety that develop when lovers leave suddenly. These women set up life-styles where they don't have to be dependent on men, and they channel their energies into their careers.

We see these dual trends reflected in popular magazines. A recent issue of *Cosmopolitan*, for example, which is targeted to women in their twenties and early thirties, featured a lead story titled "Taking Charge of Your Life Without a Man." Inside there was another article titled "How You Can Tell If He's in a Marrying Mode."[22]

In short the concept of a male shortage is not confined to women in midlife—who really do have the numbers working against them—but it has become a prevailing mind-set among many young women who are struggling with the same polarities that are pressuring more mature women: Can you really be a woman and also be successful? Or do you have to make a choice? Will men desire you if you are career-minded? And if you really make it on your own, will you respect a man who is not your professional peer?

Women of all ages are in a double bind: Unlike men, who typically define their masculinity in a variety of rituals that have nothing at all to do with females —prowess in sports, war, politics, and business— women still tend to define their womanliness through motherhood and marriage. Many of us invest men with magical powers to confer a sense of feminine self-worth on us. No matter how successful we are in our chosen fields, we still vie for male approval or attention: We dress to please men; we feel wounded if a man bypasses us for another woman or simply doesn't select us; we may feel violated if a man has sex with us and doesn't call again.

What's at stake is not simply our fragile egos— what's at stake is our feminine identity, our sexual mystique, the mysterious part of ourselves that seeks affirmation through an intimate union with a man.

"Many women who don't have a consistent relationship with a man have difficulties seeing themselves as feminine due to the lack of reflection or mirroring of that aspect of the self by a man," points out Janice S. Lieberman, a Manhattan psychoanalyst who has written and spoken extensively about the impact of the male shortage on single women. "The realistic shortage of men available to women over thirty, particularly college-educated women, intensifies these feelings of low self-esteem. Women who are single for a long time often become so frustrated by repeated episodes of abandonment, disappointment, and rejection that their self-confidence is undermined and this interacts with other intra-psychic conflicts.

"Many develop a galaxy of symptoms ranging from eating disorders to depression to insomnia. These symptoms can undermine their psychological growth and further impede their ability to effectively search for a mate. Usually, they believe that all of their symptoms will disappear when they find men to marry."[23]

Put simply, women are in a catch-22: There is a realistic shortage of men that begins to affect women when they reach their late thirties. But the real problem for women is not just the numerical shortage of men; it is the dynamics described above that play havoc with a woman's self-esteem and female identity.

This is not to say that some women don't have internal conflicts that may either block them from bonding with men or set up stresses when they do. But the male shortage tends to aggravate these conflicts instead of appeasing them, and it often creates new stresses that have nothing to do with improper nurturing, unrealistic fantasies, and the panoply of neurotic conflicts that all of us—married and single, men and women—harbor to some extent.

Why is it that some women are able to transcend these dynamics and others cave in to the pressures? Remember: Men don't marry turtles. Women don't marry antelopes. They marry each other. In 1987 almost half a million women over the age of thirty-five found spouses.

Statistics only reveal patterns. They don't have authority over your life, your ego, and your will. Don't give them a magical power they don't have. On the other hand statistics also make it clear that women who want to marry—or even date—may have to chart a course through rough waters.

We've already seen that demographics can play an important role in dating and relating. Do they also affect the specific ways in which men and women interact romantically? What are the realistic—and optimal—choices that women have in a society where low sex ratios prevail when they've been conditioned by norms that developed in societies with high sex ratios?

The Rites of Dating: Can Women Ask Men to Dance?

I f logic—rather than conditioning—governed our behavior in dating relationships, women would wine men and dine them; we'd boast about our accomplishments—and we'd use every trick in the book to woo men and marry them. After all, we are living in a time when women are striving for parity with men. We want equal salaries and jobs; we want men to share child-rearing and household chores.

Do women also want parity in romance? Do we want to take the lead in relationships—or at least share it? Do we want to split expenses on dates? Do we want men who are our peers—or men who are superior and providers as well?

More to the point, how do men feel? Are *they* responsive when a woman tries to take the lead? Or do they back off? Are men still attracted to women who are dependent, coy, and compliant, or are they attracted to women who are independent, successful, and up front about their feelings?

To answer some of these questions, I did a computer search in the New York Public Library, trying to find surveys on dating behavior today, particularly among older men and women. I found only a handful of books that focused on dating patterns at all, and even though I managed to uncover some surveys on recent dating behavior, most of these were about women of college age or in their twenties. Only a few took into account older women as well. The most all-encompassing was a survey conducted by *Cosmopolitan* magazine in 1985, which collected responses from 65,000 readers, most of them in their twenties and early thirties.[1]

As a result I developed my own six-page questionnaire on dating behavior, with the help of two survey-research specialists. I sent the questionnaire to three hundred men and three hundred women—all of them over thirty-five—who at one time had attended social events I set up for professional people in Manhattan, a core of whom had degrees from Columbia University.

I received ninety-two responses from women (roughly a 30 percent response) and fifty-four from men (a 15 percent response). Four-fifths of the women had a master's degree and a quarter had LL.B.'s, Ph.D.'s or M.D.'s as well; 15 percent had MBA's. Most were in their forties and single (never-married)—the rest had been divorced for many years. The median income was a hefty $50,000. Only thirteen women earned less than $30,000; ten earned $100,000 or more.

Most of the men were in their forties and fifties,

and more were bachelors then divorcés. Over half were lawyers, doctors, or Ph.D.'s; their median income was $75,000. Only five men earned less than $40,000 and seven men earned $200,000 or more.

Admittedly the group is not typical of men and women throughout the United States, but they represent attitudes and behavior patterns of mature men and women who live in a large city and who have been independent for many years. I have used their responses, along with the other surveys I found, as a basis for the following discussion.

Who Takes the Lead: The Tyranny of Gender

Anyone who has been single for more than five years knows that dating, as humorist Bruce Feirstein comments in *Nice Guys Sleep Alone: Dating in the Difficult Eighties*, is just about as pleasant as root canal. "We're the first generation who have dated for more than two decades," he writes, "and we still don't know how to do it."[2]

The rules today are truly blurred, and androgyny has emerged as the new operative norm. Women have the freedom to ask men out for dates, pay their own way, and assert their sexual desires without subterfuge or apology. At least that's the ideal: About two-thirds of the women and almost all the men I surveyed said that women should take as much initiative in dating as men.

"Many men are shy," explained a successful male attorney. "I have met many interesting women whom I did not notice until they became aggressive."

But there is a gap between attitude and behavior. Many women still seem to be governed by the tradition that says it's the man's responsibility and prerogative to get relationships started. Not one woman I surveyed said she called men "frequently" for first dates; only a quarter of the women said they made this gesture "sometimes," and three-fourths said they "seldom" or "never" invited men out for a first date.

Many women were even reluctant to call men for dates after they'd been out with them. Only half admitted they would call a man "sometimes" after he asked them out and over a third said they "seldom" or "never" took this step.

"Although it might be ideal to be up front, most, if not all, men need 'the chase,' " explained a school administrator in her early forties who dates frequently. "Since I'm not a game player, I try to refrain from seeming too anxious."

There's a common notion that younger women are freer about extending invitations to men than women brought up in the 1950s and '60s. Yet many still rely on men to make the moves. According to the *Cosmopolitan* survey, only 40 percent of their respondents under the age of eighteen said that they would call a man for a second date if he didn't call back after a first date, compared with only 20 percent of women in their mid-thirties who said they would.

Heather Remoff, a social scientist who surveyed the dating patterns of sixty-six women of various ages and educational levels for her book, *Sexual Choice: A Woman's Decision*, found a similar trend: When she asked women whether they preferred "Forthright Pursuit," "Situational Manipulation," "Signal Exchange," or "Veto Power" when they were interested in attracting a man, almost no one opted for the direct approach.

"A women who uses Forthright Pursuit as her initial and primary method of establishing contact with a man loses rather than gains control over such encounters," she explains. "If the male rejects her invitation, it is often very difficult for her to move to other strategies. Contact may be ended before it has a chance to begin."[3]

Timothy Perper, a Philadelphia-based biologist and anthropologist and the author of *Sex Signals*, a study of dating behavior today, surveyed about one hundred women in their twenties. He found that young women still rely on traditional female ploys—indirect gestures, flirtation, provocative clothing, and body language—to make their interest known and arouse the ardor of a man.

"Formal courtship—the domain of asking someone for a date, escorting her or wining and dining her, and even asking her to marry—is primarily still a male activity," he maintains. "By their own lights, men play the game of formal courtship quite strictly by the rules. Indeed, the closest parallel to such activities might be an immensely complex game of basketball or tennis, played as much for its own sake as in the desire to 'win the woman.' [And] men admire people who *play* by the rules and occasionally even *win* by the rules."[4]

The real question is why these rules are still operative in the social world when women are trying so hard to be treated as equals in the workplace. Do women have to play a double role, being competitive in their careers and submissive in romantic encounters?

Biology or Conditioning?

Traditional anthropologists such as Charles Darwin and Margaret Mead point out that genes are critical. Female animals, they argue, are inherently more passive, selective, and cautious in sexual encounters than males because they typically emit only one egg during ovulation. Therefore they have a biological imperative to protect themselves from the risk of pregnancy, and this causes them to be judicious about their choice of a mate. Males, on the other hand, are endowed with unlimited sperm and have a mandate to impregnate as many females as possible to perpetuate the species. As a result they are more aggressive—and less selective—about choosing sexual partners.[5]

Since human beings evolved from primates, anthropologists say that we inherited these biological differences. In primitive societies these differences turned men into hunters and warriors and females became nurturing, domestic figures. Despite the modification of these roles today males still have a need to pursue females and conquer them; females have a need to be selected and selective. They instinctively size up men as fathers—even when reproduction is not an issue. As Margaret Mead quipped in an article in *Time* magazine, "Women pick providers for sexual mates. Men pick anyone."[6] But some recent scholars have begun to dispute the notion that aggression is a sex-linked characteristic. Sarah Hrdy, for example, a primatologist at Harvard and the author of *The Woman That Never Evolved*, has found that among monkeys and apes—the primates closest to *Homo sapiens*—females are fiercely competitive, sexually aggressive, and promiscuous.[7]

Psychologists, on the other hand, argue that conditioning is the real cause of the gender distinctions that seem to set men and women apart. "At this stage of male-female interaction in our society, when a woman asks a man to dance it is for most an external gesture, a symbol, rather than a fully integrated, 'natural' response," writes Herb Goldberg, a therapist and professor of psychology at California State University, in *The Inner Male.*

"The struggle women have overtly pursuing the man they are attracted to is equivalent to men's struggle to be passive and not want to make an approach when they are strongly interested. It's no more easy for women to take control than it is for men to give up control. It is no simpler for women to transcend their fear than it is for men to acknowledge their fear. . . . As hard as it is for a man to avoid staring at an attractive woman, it is equally difficult for a woman to look directly at a man in an elevator. . . . *What seems to be easy or obvious to one sex is actually foreign, painful, and even frightening for the other, and that awareness needs to be grasped at a deeper level by both sexes, although few seem to do it.*"[8]

But gender conditioning is not the only factor—and any woman who has been kept on Call Waiting by an ambivalent suitor might dismiss the notion that there is anything at all natural about a process that tends to put men securely in the driver's seat. According to historian Beth Bailey, the real source is economics: Men are in control of dating today because they are willing—and expected—to pay for the privilege. Such was not the case years ago, she points out. Throughout the nineteenth century social meetings were largely initiated by women, who asked eligible men to afternoon teas, dinners, or dances.

"At first [a girl's] mother or guardian invited young men to call," writes Bailey. "In subsequent seasons the young lady had more autonomy and could bestow an invitation to call upon any unmarried man to whom she had been properly introduced at a private dance, dinner, or other 'entertainment.' Outside of courtship, this sort of calling was primarily a woman's activity, for *women largely controlled social life*"[9] (italics mine).

With the rise of industrialism and urban living, working girls from modest families didn't have access to fancy parlors to entertain men. Instead they met suitors in public places, where men were required to treat them. Soon enough, women from more respectable families wanted this kind of freedom and excitement. As these women began going to college or working outside the home, they rebelled against the system of parental control and began accepting invitations from men—instead of issuing them.

Independence, however, was a double-edged sword: As young women were weaned from the supervision of their parents, they became dependent on men instead. "Dating not only transformed the outward modes and conventions of American courtship, it also changed the distribution of control and power in courtship," writes Bailey.

"What men were buying in the dating system was not just female companionship, not just entertainment—but power. Money purchased obligation; money purchased inequality; money purchased control. The conventions that grew up to govern dating codified women's inequality and ratified men's power. Men asked women out; women were condemned as 'aggressive' if they expressed interest in a man too directly. . . . The dating system required men always to assume control, and women to act as men's dependents."[10]

Control or Convention?

This tradition still prevails, and the shortage of men perpetuates it because the plethora of women makes it even easier for men to take the lead. Men are reluctant to give up this power, because it would undermine their autonomy and control.

Career women have another problem as well. We have been trained to cultivate our decision-making and logical faculties. We're used to calling some of the shots some of the time. But for the most part we're still expected to play a passive role in dating, and this sets up a conflict in many women.

"I'd rather take charge because I feel more in control—and want it," says a forty-five-year-old manager. "I don't like waiting for men to call me, because it makes me feel powerless. At work I make decisions and have a lot to say in how things are run. A woman is a natural victim because she has only the freedom to reject a man instead of being able to move a relationship along. She has to be compliant or manipulative. Men are more integrated—they use in their social lives the same skills they've developed at work."

And so the myth persists: Real men pursue women and conquer them; real women are sought out and conquered. One man who sets great store by his masculine prowess explained it this way: "If I wanted you, I would pursue you. I'd invite you to dinner or breakfast or lunch or offer you a hotdog. I love the challenge of the pursuit—and the more reluctant you were, the more persistent I'd become, until I got you where I wanted you—not necessarily sexually—but until you wanted me."

Many men do back off when a woman makes a

direct overture. Some are simply not interested; others are traditional and see a woman's advances as an infringement of their male turf. Some may be so insecure about their own masculinity that they won't respect any woman who tries to woo them. When a woman comes on too strong to men with this nature and tries to corner them, she is usually destined to lose because she has violated their need to be in charge. Even if she wins, she may also lose because she may violate her own feeling that she can be valued only if she is sought out.

"Women are actively pursuing men today but often they won't admit it," says psychoanalyst Janice Lieberman. "It's humiliating for a woman to admit that she pursued a man and got him—or didn't get him."

The real problem many women are having today is not dealing with men's testy egos; it's dealing with their own insecurities, which often come into play when they assert their own needs and make direct overtures to men. Yet the reality is that many men are also insecure and they need the same kind of reinforcement that many women crave. These men may turn out to be even more responsive in relationships than men who always need to be in charge.

"I used to confuse women by my seeming indifference and not making calls in the way they thought I would if I were interested," says a lawyer who is high-powered in his work. "In fact the fear of rejection was always a factor, and when I met Nancy [the woman he married] I liked her, but I didn't want to make overtures if it was a total no-go. I wanted some indication that there was some interest on her part."

Women really do have options today to assert their emotional and sexual needs. But the key is not in developing artificial tricks or ploys that will allow a man to feel that he is taking the lead; rather, it lies in developing enough self-confidence to go after what you want without giving off the message that you are needy, dependent, and desperate.

"I had to make the first move, and that's part of what really endeared me to my husband," explained one woman. "We were friends and he played a waiting game because he was scared I would say no. But he was smart to let me come to him, because by the time I did, I knew that I really wanted him. I knew how he felt and I wasn't afraid of being rejected."

Many men, in fact, do welcome women who take the initiative; more often than not it is secure men who are responsive to these gestures. Men who feel good about their masculinity will view these openings as generous overtures that enhance their image of themselves as desirable and worthy of being sought out. Explained one man, "There's nothing so charming as a pretty woman who indicates she is interested in you."

Men who are recently divorced and who have been dependent upon their wives to set up their social schedules may even be relieved to find a woman who is willing to step in and make the first or second move. Dating may be just as foreign and frightening to them as it is to divorced women who have been insulated from the pressures of single life for many years.

"Androgyny is about options and about never having to feel helpless," says Cheryl Merser, the author of *Honorable Intentions*, who interviewed three hundred men and women of various ages throughout the United States for her book on dating customs. "The upside of androgyny is that if you're really leaning toward pizza, you have a pretty good chance of getting it. The downside is that there is no one to take charge if you can't decide between pizza and sushi. And because androgny is so new to courtship, it leaves us wondering who's supposed to do what—etiquette by trial and error."[11]

The upside, in short, is that you stand a chance of getting what you want and placating the feelings of impotency that often develop when you have to depend upon someone else to take charge. The downside is that you can get rejected and put off. But at least you'll know where you stand and you can free yourself to go on to other matters.

Who Makes the First Move?

Some studies have shown that men are more responsive to women who confront them directly than to women who confuse them with innuendoes that come across as double messages. According to a study conducted with two hundred college students in California about the lines that men and women use to meet each other in parties, supermarkets, and singles' bars, men prefer openers that are assertive and direct and demand an answer—"Hi, my name is Mary, what's yours?"—to openers that are cute or flippant and difficult to answer.[12]

Timothy Perper, who observed how men and women make contact in singles' bars, maintains that all sexual encounters involve a series of "escalation" points that begin when either a man or a woman makes an overture. It really doesn't matter who initiates the gesture; what matters is how each person responds.[13] For example he shows that a woman typically sits near a man hoping that he will talk to her. Or she may address him with a friendly remark that demands a response. ("What are you drinking?" for instance, or "Do you come here often?") If he responds, she will turn to him and listen. If conversation continues, they will begin facing each other and they may even cross the same leg or sit in the same way. Eventually she may graze his arm with her hand. He in turn will touch her arm. Soon they will be gazing into each other's eyes intently, oblivious of any other activity in the room.

As these escalation points keep occurring, the couple will continue to "synchronize" their movements and responses. Eventually they may wind up in bed, or they may merely wind up making a date for another meeting. The encounter will continue as long as each person responds to the gestures of the other. When response ceases—on either side—so will the prospect of a relationship.

"At an escalation point," says Perper, "the *partner's* behavior determines whether the interaction will continue: an overture that will increase the couple's intimacy must be emotionally *acceptable* to the other person. If it is not, intimacy cannot grow."[14]

But because we're often so focused on who is going to make the next move, we turn dates into tense tribunals and forget that the real purpose of dating is simply to explore each other—and respond naturally. And if you are confident and relaxed, you will make gestures in a way that will not make a man feel pressured, defensive, or crowded. Most men need space; most men also need empathy and reassurance.

"It's hard to find a woman who is willing to give and who is not looking for something in return," said one man. "And the only way you are going to receive is to give first. Some women have already decided what 'we' are going to do when there is only an 'I.' "

You cannot pursue a man who doesn't want to be

pursued. But you can encourage men by being open about your needs and responsive to their needs. If you truly want to get to know a man better, you owe it to yourself to take a risk and get the ball rolling. Women who don't take any initiative at all are going to perpetuate a system where they are always on Call Waiting.

Courtship Feeding: Who Pays the Dinner Check?

Initiative is one important matter. Paying the bill at dinner is another. In the beginning the rule of thumb seems to be that when a man does the asking, a man also does the paying: Four-fifths of the women in my survey said they rarely shared expenses on the first or second date. This included high-earners as well as those with more modest salaries.

Women also said that when they didn't want to see a man again, they often offered to split the check. But if they were interested in a man, they put great store in his willingness to treat them.

Sociologist Heather Remoff has one explanation: "The power of food as ritual is undoubtedly enhanced because food is so central to survival. An expensive car also serves a symbolic function for a female, but food, with its double connotation of necessity and surplus, has a much more direct relationship to an actual sexual response. . . . Women fall in love with men who feed them."[15]

Conversely men may fall in love with women who feed *them*: According to some modern etiquette makers, when a woman makes the first gesture and asks a man out, she should be willing to pay the bill. "A woman is free to ask a man for a first date, but if she does she should pay everything, including tickets, taxi or parking charges and coat check," advises Letitia Baldrige, the author of *Letitia Baldrige's Complete Guide to the New Manners for the 1990's.*[16]

Dating costs money. Dating is expensive. Dining out once a week in New York or even Dallas can cost anywhere from fifty to a hundred dollars for two people. Some men can afford these expenses easily—particularly if they can write them off as a business expense. Many men don't have this luxury, and many are supporting ex-wives, children, and elderly parents as well.

Yet many women are still conflicted about sharing expenses, even when a relationship stabilizes. A third of the women in my survey said they wouldn't share any expenses at all in an ongoing relationship, and this included some very high-earners. A third said they would—and a third said it depended on a man's income: If a man earned the same as they did or less, they would be willing to share. But if a man earned more, they expected him to pay all the expenses most of the time or most of the expenses all of the time.

Just about everyone, however, said that in marriage they would pool all resources. Almost no one expected a man to pay for all major expenses. The reason for this apparent discrepancy may be that courtship is still a ritual—a time when people are testing each other. One of the ways that women typically assess a man's devotion and protective instincts is through his willingness to treat them well. When marriage occurs and a woman knows that a man is committed to her, she's more willing to share her assets with her husband.

AIDS and Sex: The Retreat
of the One-Night Stand?

If many men and women are old-fashioned when it comes to money and setting up dates, our libidos don't stand on ceremony anymore. Over half the people I surveyed (men and women combined) said that they'd had sex with their most recent boyfriend or girlfriend on or by the third date. Only a few people hopped into bed on the first date—and only a few waited longer than four dates.

Just about everyone in the group—men as well as women—said they were more conservative today about casual sex than they were five years ago. Both sexes said that AIDS was one of the inhibiting factors. Many said that they were more selective about partners now and that they waited longer to have sex. Two-thirds of the women said that they asked their partners to use condoms, and three-fifths of the men said that they used condoms with new partners. Even so, almost half the women said that they would have sex with men without using condoms, if they trusted the men and were confident about their sexual histories.

"I know my partners and trust them—and we discuss sexual partners or the lack of them," said a professor who had had sex with two different men during a six-month period.

Shelley Juran, a psychologist at Pratt Institute in Brooklyn, New York, found a similar trend. She surveyed over one hundred men and one hundred women of varying ages whom she met in singles' bars in Greenwich Village, a neighborhood where the fear of AIDS runs high, since it is heavily populated with gay men. Eighty percent of her respondents said their behavior had changed since Surgeon General C. Everett Koop came out with his recommendation that people should use condoms. Over a third of the women and men said that they insisted on condoms now, and many said that they were having casual sex less frequently. But more women than men said that they were likely to query their partners about their previous sexual partners.

"Among heterosexuals, casual sex is decreasing at a rapid rate as the potential consequences of a sexual encounter have become lethal, although this is unlikely," Juran concludes. "Condom use has increased dramatically among this group, and for many people the spontaneous casual sexual experiences of the sexual revolution are either over or have been greatly curtailed and modified."[17]

The specter of AIDS, however, is only one factor that has modified sexual behavior. Many women and men I queried said that the desire for a long-term partner and real intimacy in sex were equally important.

Yet many men said that they still enjoyed casual sex. Most women said that they didn't enjoy it. This may be one reason why the men I surveyed had more sexual partners during a six-month period than the women I surveyed. These men also dated twice as many new partners during that time period as women did and spent shorter periods of time between relationships.

A third of the women were dating someone regularly when they answered the questionnaire; a sixth said that they'd had no dates at all in a six-month period. Among those who were dating, most had only one sexual partner during a six-month period. Only four had three partners or more. Two-thirds said that their last important relationship had taken place a year ago or earlier. (Incidentally women who earned over $50,000 went out as much—or as little—as women in lower-income brackets. There was virtually no difference in the patterns of single and divorced women.)

In contrast two-thirds of the men were dating a woman regularly when they answered the questionnaire; only four men said they'd had no dates at all during a six-month period; only a third had one sexual partner during this period of time. A third had three or more sexual partners, and a couple of men had as many as ten. Only a third said that their most important relationship had occurred a year ago or earlier.

Another reason for these differences is demographics. Due to the male shortage most women have fewer dates than men do. Many women are also reluctant to set up dates when men don't make the first move. But there's another factor as well. Men, for the most part, are willing to have sex with any woman who excites their ardor; woman tend to be more hesitant, because they can't so easily separate their sexual yearnings from their desire to give love and receive it. As a result the shortage of men nowadays puts women in a double bind: Many feel pressured to sleep with men as soon as possible for fear they will lose them if they don't; yet many also know that sleeping with a man readily can have the opposite effect.

"They want sexual relationships, not serious ones," said one *Cosmopolitan* participant. "And if you give them sex, you never hear from them again! If you don't, they think you're playing games and probably won't call again either. Figure men!"

Yet almost all the men in my survey said they would call a woman again if she said it was "too soon" to have sex. When men are accommodated too quickly, they often lose interest—or they become frightened that they have made some kind of commitment they're not ready to honor.

"Men who come on real quick are often not available emotionally," points out Robin Ashman, a New York City therapist. "Men who want to get to know you don't come on so strong so fast, and they are more careful in the beginning. The men who want to get into bed fast want excitement, but not long-term relationships."

Men tend to prize women who prize themselves. And if flesh is what you're selling, flesh is what a man's going to buy. A man who is really responsive will pace his sexual interest to yours. Men who aren't willing to do this in the beginning of a relationship will probably not be responsive later on.

Marriage: An Ideal in Flux

For many people the real goal of dating is marriage. As Timothy Perper points out, the central icon of the singles scene is neither casual sex nor even casual relationships, but commitment and its handmaidens: intimacy, love, stability, and finally marriage. "Being single has become a metaphor for a general social malaise and of a general failure of life to provide a stable, central core around which everything else is built," he writes. "In the tragic ethos of the singles scene . . . people believe that a normal and productive life should be a *married* life, and that if marriage is not forthcoming, then something is deeply wrong, not only with the individual but with society itself."[18]

Three-quarters of the men I surveyed—and almost

all of the women—said they preferred marriage as a life-style. Those who didn't opted for exclusive dating relationships more frequently than cohabitation; only a few men said they preferred steady but nonexclusive relationships as a way of life. Almost everyone said their chief incentive for marrying was a "desire for intimacy" and "desire for companionship now"— more important than companionship later on or a steady sex life. The desire to share chores and expenses was the least important reason. And this represents a real change from the past.

Up until recent times almost all women married men who would provide them with financial support, status in the community, and children. Men, in turn, married women who would take care of their homes and give them sons—or daughters—to carry on their lineage. Love, passion, and even companionship were subordinate to these other needs. Nowadays the entry of women into the work force and the acceptance of extramarital affairs has redefined the parameters of marriage. We still crave the sense of belonging, the well-being, the good life, that marriage is supposed to provide, but as demographer Robert Schoen notes, the "marital union" of the past is giving way to the "marital partnership" of the future, in which spouses will be more egalitarian and less dependent.[19]

Almost all the men and women I interviewed said that they wanted spouses who could share their interests and be supportive. In my survey men as well as women said that "intelligence" and "sexual fidelity" were the most important qualities they wanted in a mate. They also valued the ability to be communicative, emotionally supportive, and affectionate. Successful careers and earning power, however, were not critical to either gender.

Only a quarter of the women said that "success"

and "good income" were extremely important in a potential mate. Over half the women said that they would marry men who were *less* successful in their careers than they were—and high-earning women were even less concerned about a man's earning power than women with moderate salaries.

Even more surprising, 90 percent of the men said they would marry women who were *more* successful than they were.

"I'm secure in my own profession and am not threatened by a woman who is successful," commented a physician. "I'd be proud of her accomplishments."

Why some women still prefer men who are more —or at least equally—successful may have less to do with conditioning than the fact that successful men often give ambitious women more freedom to explore their own talents.

"The feminist emphasis on egalitarian relationships has left some confusion in its wake," points out Remoff. "An emphasis on strength in men is not to compensate for some lack of strength in women. On the contrary, having a strong male partner very often frees a woman to express her own power. Truly powerful men do not keep women down."[20]

We may still seek partners who will complement us in critical ways, but we are learning to respond to inner needs instead of paying heed to the gender polarities we were all conditioned to respect as the basis for romantic attachments. Assertive women may be happiest with men who are not competitive; nurturing women may seek out men who need to be nurtured; female executives may be drawn to struggling artists—and blondes are often drawn to brunettes.

"My husband has some traits we associate with women. He's volatile and extremely emotional and cries more than I do," explained one woman. "I have some masculine traits—I'm more rooted and know how to handle problems. He admires me and values my mind. And he demands a lot from me, which makes me feel I have more to give."

The upside of these new ideals is that many of us look for mates who will satisfy interior needs rather than external ones. The downside is that interior needs are often unclear. Finding a spouse who will provide intimacy, enhance self-growth, and fill our yearnings for happiness often imposes pressures and expectations that are simply unrealistic and impossible to attain. "The American marriage ideal is one of the most conspicuous examples of hitching our wagon to a star," said Margaret Mead in *Male and Female*. "It is one of the most difficult marriage forms that the human race has ever attempted."[21]

John Welwood states that the challenge facing couples nowadays is finding a synthesis between our need for belonging or commitment and our need to be true to ourselves as individuals. If we really want our relationships to work out, we have to respect ourselves and we also have to be realistic about what we want or need from a partner.[22]

One reason mature men and women have a better chance of creating sustaining unions is that they are more experienced and in touch with their own needs than younger people who are still shaping their own identities. When you are truly self-reliant and centered, you will be more capable of selecting a partner who will enhance your ability to grow—and give love freely—because you won't be driven by panic, anxiety, or a need to define your own self-worth through another person.

"You marry differently at this age," explained a mother who remarried at forty-seven. "When I married for the first time, I had a sense that my fate was wound up with my husband. If *he* wasn't going any-place, *I* wasn't going anyplace. But I've learned that extremely aggressive and successful men are not so easy to live with—they're not so good up close.

"I still like being married; I like a team; I like help-ing out and being helped; I like entertaining together. The difference is that now I have a better sense of myself. I have my own money, my own friends, my own life-style, and it's lovely to work with someone, but I don't need a man to make me a person. I'm okay on my own."

Women may not have as many options as men to pursue whom they want in the way of romantic part-ners. But we do have the option to know who we are and what we can offer. Also, we have the freedom to reject stereotypes that constrain our ability to act. When we begin to dismiss conventions that restrict our choices, we will find many more men available.

She's Older— He's Younger: Turning the Male Shortage Around

- *Forty-one* percent of brides age thirty-five to forty-four married younger men in 1987.[1]

- Thirty-five-year-old women married almost as many thirty-year-old men as forty-year-old men.

- Fifty-year-old brides married more men in their forties than men in their sixties.

- *Eight* percent of fifty-year-old grooms married women who were thirty or younger—*17* percent married women who were fifty or older.

- A forty-five-year-old woman is 1.5 times more likely to marry a man in his forties than a man in his fifties.

- *0.003* percent of twenty-five-year-old brides marry men in their fifties and sixties.

Most of us have grown up believing that a romance between an older woman and a younger man is as rare as a snowstorm in July—the exclusive privilege of women with extraordinary wealth, charisma, and sex appeal, who often live in Hollywood. Sigourney Weaver, Raquel Welch, Jacqueline Bisset, Barbra Streisand, Mary Tyler Moore, Goldie Hawn, and Bette Midler are just some of the well-known actresses who have teamed up with younger men.

Statistics now reveal that these women are no longer exceptions to the rule. Thousands of American women who are not famous, exceptionally beautiful, or rich are following suit. In doing so they are responding to the mandates of feminist dogma that have empowered women with a new freedom to identify their needs and act upon them. Many women are now selecting younger partners—*not because they are younger* but because they are *appropriate* and fulfill their deepest needs.

◆

Between 1970 and 1987 the percentage of women marrying younger men almost doubled. In 1970 only a sixth of women were marrying younger men; nowadays almost a quarter of American women are doing so. More to the point, this trend is prevalent only among mature women, who tend to be more restricted in the marriage market than younger women. Between 1970 and 1987 the percentage of women age thirty-five to forty-four who married younger men *increased* from 34.5 percent to 41.2 percent, and the percentage of women age forty-five to fifty-four who married younger men also increased slightly from 34.4 percent to 35.6.[2]

In contrast younger women are continuing to marry "up." Statistics show that only an eighth of women in their early twenties—and roughly a quarter of women in their late twenties—are marrying younger men. And there are no signs that either pattern will change. In the future we can expect to find that even more women in their late thirties and forties will be marrying men who are younger than they are.

In doing so, these women are practicing, unconsciously or consciously, what demographers have been preaching for some time: The only viable way to overcome the male shortage that limits women's choices in midlife is for women to marry younger men. "In order to bring the social system in accord with biological reality, it would be necessary to change age patterns at marriage drastically," maintains Davor Jedlicka, a sociologist at the University of Georgia who has studied the phenomenon.

"On the average, wives would have to be seven years older than their husbands. Both men and women would then have equal chances in mate selection, and average differences in life expectancy of either surviving spouse would be less than one year. *Only a small portion of unmarried older women [will] succeed in mate selection as long as it is acceptable for older men to marry younger women while at the same time it is taboo for older women to seek, date and marry younger men*"[3] (italics mine).

The Statistical Puzzle

One reason we've been influenced to think that almost all women marry older men—particularly older women who are disadvantaged in the marriage market—is that reporters writing on the issue tend to cite the marriage patterns of *men* instead of citing the marriage patterns of *women.*

And it may sound like a contradiction, but most men do marry younger women: Over 80 percent of men in their late forties and fifties are marrying younger women these days; only about 12 percent are marrying women older than they are.[4]

Even so, the age gap between these men and their spouses is not nearly so great as many of us have been led to believe. Most men in midlife select wives who are relatively close to them in age, and only a handful of them select women who are fifteen or twenty years younger. The average age difference between a forty-five-year-old man, for example, and his younger spouse is only six years, and the average gap between a fifty-five-year-old man and his younger bride is seven and a half years.

At the same time, 40 percent of women in their late thirties and forties are also marrying younger grooms. Although most of these men are merely one to five years younger than their brides, many women are marrying men who are ten to fifteen years younger as well.

Why don't the statistics match up? If 80 percent of men are marrying younger women, why aren't 80 percent of women marrying older men? Because both sexes are dipping into larger—and younger—pools of unmarried people for mates. As a result the *percentage* of older men and women marrying "down" is always greater in midlife than the *percentage* of younger men and women marrying "up."

Visualize two pyramids: The top of one pyramid contains unmarried women in their forties; the bottom contains unmarried men in their thirties. If twenty women from the top marry twenty men from the bottom, the percentage of women in their forties marrying men in their thirties is greater than the percentage of men in their thirties marrying women in their forties.

The same formula works for men. The top of the other pyramid contains unmarried men in their forties; the bottom contains unmarried women in their thirties. If twenty men from the top marry twenty women from the bottom, the percentage of older men marrying younger women is greater than the percentage of younger women marrying older men.

These are the statistical facts: Women are beginning to show the same behavior patterns as men when it comes to selecting spouses. Even though the motivations that govern these preferences may differ somewhat for each gender, the important point to keep in mind is that women are finally reversing the traditional age patterns that have put them at a disadvantage.

"Whether Jeffrey Fever [the union of older women and younger men] in women is a response to the dearth of available middle-aged men, or less a response than an active, conscious choice by women, is not clear," writes Barbara Gordon in her recent book, *Jennifer Fever*, a study of older men and younger women. "It may also be the result of the evaporation of sexual taboos that usually blanket such relationships. Whatever the reasons, women are doing it and both they and their younger lovers are happy to talk about it."[5]

The Rites of Marrying "Up"

Since these are the facts, why do so many savvy women who want to marry think that their only choice is to compete for men who are out to pasture instead of setting their sights on younger men?

Media hype is one reason. Despite the celebrity of various media stars over forty—Diane Sawyer, Gloria Steinem, Elizabeth Taylor, Jane Fonda, and Cher—who have shown that age is no deterrent to sex appeal, romantic leads for mature female stars are still few, and actresses are rarely, if ever, cast with actors who are clearly younger than they are.

In contrast male movie stars in their fifties and even sixties—Paul Newman, Robert Redford, Jack Nicholson, and Jack Lemmon—are often sought out for roles where a romantic intrigue with a young woman is part of the script. James Bond in his heyday almost always wound up in bed with a woman who defied conventional norms: in one film she was black; in some she was married or a spy from the other side, but she was never older.

We are all affected by these scenarios. Read any Personals column and you will find scores of ads by men in their fifties seeking women who are in their twenties or early thirties. But it's rare to find a woman in her forties advertising for a man in his twenties or even his thirties.

"You inherit cultural images from books and movies and television," points out an artist in his early twenties, who recently married a woman in her forties. "Mom's always a little shorter, and younger; the boy is born first; you live in a suburban home; and Dad goes out and makes money. Media images are exclusionary and build up expectations of what you can and can't achieve. If you're expected to behave this way—and don't—chances are that you will be disappointed."

Before I began doing research for this book and discovered that almost half the women I was interviewing had married younger men, I, too, was governed by these norms. Whenever I found myself on a date with a man who turned out to be younger than I was, I would feel self-conscious, embarrassed, and even silly. Sometimes I'd go out of my way to avoid the issue of age altogether. Or I'd fudge about the year I graduated from college, the year I settled in New York, the year I began publishing. I turned my younger brother into my older brother, and sometimes, of course, I tripped up because I'd talk glibly about loafers, bobby socks, circle pins, and Uncle Miltie on TV.

Most of the time my dates didn't care. But I knew and I cared. I thought I'd be found out and dismissed. After all, I was reared in a traditional society where it was the norm for women to pair up with older men. When I was in high school, all the boys my own age seemed immature and childish. I never thought about them as romantic partners. Later, as a student at Barnard College in the 1960s, most of my classmates routinely dated slightly older men. When we were freshmen, we dated juniors or seniors. When we were juniors and seniors, we went to mixers with students from Columbia Law School and Medical School; occasionally we even dated men who were out and working in the world.

It seemed *de rigueur* to date—and marry—men who were two to five years older than we were. We were, after all, bright women. We valued men who were more experienced than we were, more affluent, and more knowledgeable. How could you look up to a man if you were twenty-three and he was twenty-one? We simply thought that's the way it should be.

And for centuries and centuries that's the way it was. Eve was younger than Adam because she was born out of Adam's rib. Their union became the archetypical model for all succeeding marriages. Husbands were supposed to be older, dominant, and wise; wives were younger, submissive, and innocent. Abraham—the father of the Hebraic tribes—was ten years older than his wife Sarah. Joseph was older than Mary. Napoleon was older than Josephine. And John F. Kennedy was older than Jackie.

To be sure, in ancient times there were some pragmatic reasons for these age patterns. Women were expected to bear many children. Since many infants —and wives as well—died in childbirth or soon after, women had to marry early to take full advantage of their fertility. Men, however, could be fruitful and multiply until their twilight years. Young women often desired them because they were powerful and rich. As the Greek dramatist Aristophanes stated, a woman's time was short, but a man, though gray-bearded, could always get a wife.[6]

Throughout Western civilization the median age of first marriages reflected these norms. Even when it fluctuated in response to economic factors, brides were almost always younger than their husbands. Women didn't have societal permission to marry younger men. To do so was to flaunt convention and risk censure or ridicule.

In eighteenth-century Europe women tended to marry relatively late in life—in their late twenties— because most men could not afford to take care of a family until their thirties.[7] In colonial America, however, plentiful land made it easier to amass resources more quickly, and younger marriages became the norm. In 1900 the median age of a first marriage was 25.9 for men and 21.9 for women.

Then the median age of first marriages began to fall, and it reached a low point in the 1950s, as a reaction to years of war and depression. Still, the age pattern remained the same: Women were younger than their husbands, and even in families where women worked, men were expected to be the primary providers.

"The husband was usually expected to be the economic provider, and his value in society was determined by his worth in that role," state Philip Blumstein and Pepper Schwartz, sociologists and coauthors of *American Couples*, a major research study undertaken in the 1980s. "[Even] in working-class families, the prospective groom was required to have steady employment or to earn an income equal to or better than the bride's father."[8]

Census data also show that when men marry at later ages, the age gap between spouses widens. In nineteenth-century Ireland, where poor soil made it difficult for men to develop enough assets to take care of a family, men married in their mid- to late thirties.[9] Women married in their mid- to late twenties. In early twentieth-century England the average widower married a woman who was five to ten years younger than he was.[10]

Despite all the changes that have occurred in our society, these patterns have remained. Custom, however, is now the sole reason for these age differences because the rationales that set them in motion are now largely irrelevant. Nowadays less than 1 percent of women die due to childbirth; only 1 percent of infants die within a year of birth.[11] The average mother has only two children, and she can defer child bearing until her thirties or even her forties.

Nor is earning power age-related any longer but rather a function of profession and expertise. A twenty-five-year-old lawyer usually earns more than a thirty-year-old teacher; a twenty-eight-year-old doctor may earn more than a fifty-five-year-old middle manager, and young people who are peaking in their professions typically earn more than seasoned adults who are phasing out.

However we still live in a culture where youth and power exist as competing priorities—and these qualities are gender-related. Youth and its handmaidens —beauty, innocence, naiveté, passivity, and unsoiled virtue—are considered desirable feminine traits. Power and its court jesters—affluence, maturity, experience, knowledge, responsibility, and authority— are viewed as desirable masculine traits. Most of us are still trying to reconcile these polarities, at every phase of our growth. "The Young/Old polarity—the splitting of Young and Old, and the effort to reintegrate them—is *the* polarity of human development," writes Daniel J. Levinson, a psychologist at Yale and the chief author of *The Seasons of a Man's Life*, a major research study on the psychological stages men go through as they age.[12]

Many men who are coping with a midlife crisis often seek young women as sexual partners to offset their fears of aging and prove that they are still virile. Women, however, don't have the same societal permission to allay the inevitable march of time by cultivating young lovers. The beast, in other words, can still court young beauties—but can a middle-aged women court a young Adonis?

"Refashioning the image of the middle-aged woman

into a lusty, sexually alive creature will take some doing," notes Barbara Gordon. "She knows the words society has devised to describe her: hag, witch, shrike, harridan, shrew, virago.

"But the image of the midlife male has always been of someone living in a perpetual prime. Impervious to time, he remains, regardless of his age, the energetic star forever appearing in the main event of his life. . . . Older, wiser, the lines on his face are hard-earned creases that are part of his allure, assets that contribute to his craggy charm."[13]

Vanitas vanitatis.

I recently had dinner with a divorced friend in her late forties. She is a successful consultant, extremely attractive and personable, who single-handedly raised three happy, healthy children, yet she was complaining about the men she was meeting who were in their fifties. When I advised her to seek younger men instead, she was aghast.

"Why would a younger man be interested in me when even a man in his late fifties can take out a woman who is thirty-five?" she lamented.

Why indeed?

The Spell of Social Taboos

Most of us have internalized these social taboos, and they are so deeply ingrained that many women do not even consider younger men as potential lovers or spouses. "If a woman is surprised, flattered and happy when a professional relationship with a younger man begins to turn personal, the intensity of her pleasure is soon tempered with fear: a fear of abandonment, of looking foolish, an ambivalent feeling toward making a commitment because the odds seem stacked against them as a couple," writes Virginia Houston in *Loving a Younger Man.* "She faces a series of complex concerns that range from losing her attractiveness to misgivings about her sexuality to worrying what colleagues and friends will think."[14]

◆

When Helen Thompson, a forty-two-year-old businesswoman with red hair, brown eyes, and a perky personality, met Tony, a twenty-eight-year-old economist, who had recently emigrated to the United States from Italy, she never even thought twice about him as a romantic possibility, even though he was good-looking, outgoing, and seemed interested in her. She was reared in a traditional family in Nashville, and she always dated men who were at least seven years older than she was. Her most serious beaux were ten to twelve years older.

"I always thought older men were more mature and could take care of me. I didn't even feel comfortable if a man was two or three months younger than I was," she relates. "I wanted a man who was ahead of me professionally and I expected a man to pay for everything. It made me feel more feminine."

As a result she selected men who were older, but they frustrated her needs for love and reassurance. One important man controlled her by being evasive, noncommittal, and highly critical. Another suitor would never make dates until the last minute. Once when she went ahead and made a date with another man for a Saturday night, he persuaded her to break the date. Then he refused to see her that Saturday. She blew up and ended the relationship. Four months later she invited Tony to a small dinner party.

"Tony brought me a present and flowers, and as

he was leaving, he took my hand, and I couldn't let him go," she recalls. "I was like a little baby who grabs the finger of someone and hangs on—and he stayed the night."

After that she began seeing Tony almost every day, but she denied there was any real romance between them. When she got sick one week, he came over and took care of her. Three weeks later he moved in.

Even so, it took her a while to tell friends about Tony. She fibbed about his age. "I was tickled that someone so much younger was interested in me, but I was embarrassed about the age difference. I also worried that he would be attracted to younger women." As time went on, Helen realized that Tony was more nurturing and reliable than her former boyfriends. He was eager to meet her friends and family; he wanted her full-time attention; and he was the one who initiated discussions on marriage. He made her feel secure and loved.

"He likes to do everything together and enjoys being in a home environment," she says. "He doesn't even like it when I work after hours. He's very attentive to my needs—which often seem greater than his—and he wants to make me happy and satisfied. I wonder now where he's been all my life. It's extraordinary. He feels that women his age don't know what they want or who they are. He sees me as someone who is more comfortable and more settled.

"He has a very clear idea of who he is, where he is going, and where he has come from—and he's focused on building his career, not retiring. In that respect we're really in the same place. Where you are in life can be a big problem. That was one of the main tensions with one of my former boyfriends. He was ready to retire and I was intent on building my career. Tony is also building his career, and even though I earn more money than he does, he's young and vital and has the potential to earn. He's been helpful to me in my business and advises me on how to bring in more money.

"I can't worry about the age difference because if I do, I'll drive myself crazy. Even if you're the same age as a man or ten years younger, the man can go off in a different direction. I might live until I'm eighty—and who knows if he'll make it to sixty-five? I'm happier than I've ever been. I'm calm and assured, and if anything happens, I know that I can be alone and survive. I know I can find another man. But right now I don't want to. I don't want this to end."

"My God, It's Mrs. Robinson!"

When Dustin Hoffman found himself making love to a middle-aged woman in the film *The Graduate*, some men laughed and others winced—particularly if they grew up in the 1940s and '50s. Many of these men were initiated into the rites of sexual mysteries by an older woman who was used to luring young men into her bed and teaching them what to do. In those days nice girls didn't. Having sex outside of marriage was taboo for women from respectable families.

But men were expected to have sexual experiences before they married, and they also expected their brides to be less experienced than they were. Partly because of this tradition many men who are in their fifties still want a younger woman—she seems purer and less experienced sexually than they are.

Men brought up in the feminist era may not have these same expectations, but for many of them an older woman symbolizes a mothering figure. She triggers unconscious conflicts that a younger woman is less likely to set off. "An older woman often represents a mother figure, and men usually try to repress their Oedipal urges. When a man finds that he's attracted to an older woman he feels uncomfortable because he's broken a cardinal taboo. He feels more virile and dominant with a younger woman, even if she's only slightly younger," says John Shaffer, a therapist and psychology professor at Queens College in New York City.

◆

"The idea of going out with a forty-three-year-old woman was so off the scope that I couldn't treat it seriously," recalls Richard Barkin, a thirty-three-year-old lawyer, trained at Harvard, who recently married Patricia Walton, a forty-three-year-old city planner, trained at Yale.

"I had never really conceived of marrying a woman who was ten years older. She might not be able to have children, and we might grow at different rates sexually and physiologically. A sixty-year-old woman doesn't run around as much as a fifty-year-old woman."

There were other differences as well. Richard is short and Jewish; Pat is tall and Protestant. He was raised in New York City. She was born in the South.

Pat, in fact, wasn't Richard's "ideal" type, and when he met her at a casual dinner party, he wasn't particularly interested in her. But she liked him and she made up an excuse to call him the following week. He talked to her politely on the phone, and then he said good-bye. Two weeks later he had an extra ticket for the opera. On a whim he called Pat. He knew she was older than he was, but he thought the difference was only seven years. Besides, he simply wanted a date for the opera.

The evening was pleasant, but Richard didn't call Pat for another date. So Pat took the bull by the horns and asked Richard to a party. After the party they necked in the backseat of his car. Soon after, a friend told Richard Pat's real age. He was taken aback, but he decided to go forward anyway.

"I didn't want to go ahead if it was a red light," he says. "I didn't want to make a total jackass of myself —but she was clearly interested. And by that time I really liked her."

On their next date they made plans to take a trip. Pat also initiated a sexual encounter, and things took a rocky turn. Richard wasn't ready. He couldn't perform. "I knew she wouldn't take no for an answer," he says. "I also knew I wouldn't be able to do it. That's when we had our first real catastrophe. I called her the next morning because I wanted to assure her that it had to do with me—not her—I didn't want her to feel it was a rejection. And I wanted to go away with her."

On the trip their relationship deepened. They discovered that they really enjoyed just being together and doing funky things. But sex was still a problem. When Richard complained that he was in real physical pain, Pat urged him to see a doctor when they returned. He was reluctant, but agreed. His problem turned out to be testicular and was easily cured.

Even before the problem was resolved, they both decided that they wanted to continue the relationship. On the plane ride back they began talking in terms of a serious involvement, yet they also skirted around the age issue. Pat was afraid to tell Richard how old she really was for fear of losing him. Richard knew, but didn't say anything.

By the time they discussed it openly, the age difference was no longer relevant. Richard was falling deeply in love, and ten weeks later he proposed. Then Pat began pulling back.

"I was probably deeper in love than Pat at that point," he says. "And the disparity in our romantic intensity created a problem that required working out. That became the real issue, and not our ages.

"I don't care that much about society's view—I don't usually do things to please other people. I can't think of one time I've been with Pat and considered her older. And no one I'd ever met fit the bill as well as she did—she is sexy, funny, pretty, warm, and kind.

"The main thing was that I could communicate with her better than with other women. We had a commitment to each other and we were willing to deal with problems. I could really trust her. I decided that I'd only meet someone like Pat rarely—if ever—and she was too good to pass up."

The Rights of Marrying "Down"

Having children can surface as an important issue when a man gets involved with a woman who has limited time in which to have a family. But that's just about the only practical constraint that might inhibit May-September marriages. If logic—rather than habit—governed the way we selected partners, even men in their twenties would marry "up" and women in their twenties would marry "down."

The reason is simple enough: According to NCHS women outlive men by approximately seven years. A forty-year-old woman who marries a fifty-year-old man can expect to be widowed for seventeen years if the marriage survives; a forty-five-year-old woman who marries a fifty-year-old man can expect to be on her own for twelve years.

"Age preferences at marriage have no basis in biological differences between sexes," writes Professor Jedlicka. "On the contrary, *women live longer in every developed country in the world.* They are healthier and if suicide, homicide and auto accidents are an indication of emotional stability for a category of people, then females are also far more emotionally stable."[15]

Many women also wind down physically more slowly than men do. They often have more energy than men who are their peers, and many say that they prefer younger men for this simple reason.

"I was usually attracted to men my own age or younger men, partly because I like to do a lot of young things and look younger than my age," says a forty-two-year-old publicist who recently married a thirty-three-year-old engineer she met at a summer resort. "John and I both like to ski and jog, and men in their forties and fifties often can't keep up with me. Even John has a hard time because I'm an expert skier and go on slopes that many men avoid, and I even outjog John. We have similar energy levels when we travel and similar interests as well."

Oddly enough, primates are more savvy about these issues than many *Homo sapiens.* Primatologist Sarah Hrdy points out that male monkeys almost never abandon their female partners for young monkeys. They have a preference for older mates. "There is a difference between humans and nonhumans with regard to the attraction of older males to younger females," she writes. "For humans there is infatuation with nubility, and the standard of beauty is youthfulness at the beginning of adulthood. This is not true for primates. Male primates are not attracted to younger female primates. They prefer middle-aged, older, or 'dominant' females. These females are more experienced and their infants have the highest survival rates, which would be a principal motivation on the part of the male."[16]

Why don't men behave like chimps—instead of chumps?

Sexuality is another factor that makes it logical for older women to team up with younger men. It's well documented that a woman reaches her sexual prime in her late thirties or forties. This is due to the fact that as a woman ages, the network of veins in her genitalia increases and this heightens her responsiveness.

Along with this, her hormonal levels change as she matures, which increases her sexual desire. Her androgens—male hormones—can't be produced while her estrogen levels are high early in life, but her estrogen levels begin to ebb in midlife. As they do, the androgens exert more influence and heighten her sexual urges. Even though declining estrogen levels may interfere with her lubricity—a condition that often occurs in the fifties, when menopause sets in—these problems can be resolved through simple medication that will facilitate expression of her increasing libidinal urges.

In contrast men are the most virile in their twenties, and, as they age, their potency begins to wane. Men in their fifties often experience erectile problems that are not dealt with so easily. Even if the cause is physiological—and not psychological—the mere experience or specter of impotency is so upsetting to most men that it almost always sets up anxieties that are difficult to dispel.

As Daniel Levinson points out, "When the splitting of power and weakness takes an extreme form, a man regards any sign of weakness in himself as intolerably feminine and dangerous. He goes to great lengths to deny its existence. His anxiety is heightened by every sign of biological and social decline at mid-life."[17]

Since waning potency is for most men the most severe sign of biological decline, men who experience it may gravitate toward younger women because it's easier to mask their difficulties with women who are sexually inexperienced. But men who are sexually active may find older women more compatible.

Men who don't want children may also consider older women a plus because they have either resolved the childbearing issue or their children are grown up and self-sufficient.

"I didn't want a much younger woman because I didn't want more children—and younger women usually want children," said a forty-four-year-old divorced father, who married a forty-six-year-old single woman. "I wanted a woman who could share my life experiences and my feelings about the theater. I didn't want to be a baby-sitter."

Economics can also weight the scales. Women who don't want children or women with grown children are more likely to share expenses on an ongoing basis than women who might want time off from their careers to raise a family. Money, in short, is alluring. Women have known that for a long time. Now men are finding it out and viewing potential partners accordingly.

"Susan has a career and she takes a lot of the burden off me," said a thirty-six-year-old journalist who married a thirty-nine-year-old advertising executive. "I don't have to be the sole breadwinner anymore."

Virtually all of the men I interviewed said they didn't want a woman who was completely dependent on them. Men who were going through a transition in their work were even more adamant about the point. "I'm a consultant and in a transition phase," explained a forty-seven-year-old marketing representative who married a forty-nine-year-old sales director. "I don't feel the pressure to make a lot of money because I'm no longer the only earner. Marjorie earns more than I do. In my previous marriage I had a tremendous obligation to support the family because my wife never worked, and I had to take a lot of jobs I didn't like just to make more money."

In fact economics may turn out to be one of the most significant factors in reversing traditional marriage-age patterns. "Sociologists often imply that husbands do not derive any glory from a wife's success," state Blumstein and Schwartz who surveyed about four thousand couples for their study.

"This is not generally true for the husbands in our study. *Husbands with successful wives are happier with their marriages.* These are usually men who have chosen to be in a marriage where the woman is free to pursue her career fully, and neither partner is threatened at the prospect of sharing the provider role."[18]

Overcoming the Gender Gap

In fact not all men are comfortable with women who are high earners. According to Blumstein and Schwartz, even in marriages in which women are equal earners, some men are reluctant to give women equal say in making decisions. But this seems to be truer for men who grew up in the prefeminist era, when it was neither stylish nor acceptable for women to have careers.

As one man in his fifties related, "I grew up in a generation where I was insulted if a woman paid for anything—it would be a negative reflection on me and meant I didn't have the income to take care of her."

Men who still invest a lot of their ego in their ability to pay all the bills are often threatened by career women. Therapists point out that this is another reason many middle-aged men are attracted to younger females. "The reason older men leave their wives for younger women is not, as is commonly believed, primarily to enhance sexual potency, but rather because the middle-aged wife now refuses to live in her husband's shadow.... [They seek instead] a still dependent, still adoring younger woman. Through her, these older men hope to both live out and cordon off the discrepant, questionable aspect of their own nature," says David Gutmann, a Manhattan psychiatrist, in *Jennifer Fever*.[19]

Men who were conditioned by the egalitarian ideals of feminism tend to be more comfortable with women who can pay their own way. Many put less stock in power based on status or earnings, and they have learned to define their masculinity in terms of their ability to be nurturing partners instead of authority figures. As Dr. Shaffer points out, it's often easier for a professional woman in her forties to develop a compatible relationship with a younger man. He is not as hampered by traditional taboos and may not feel threatened by her success.

◆

When Donald Blane met Miriam, his wife, he was only twenty-three and had just moved to Chicago from a small town in Ohio. She was forty, a highly paid marketing executive, and her brown hair was streaked with gray. They met at a party—she thought he was a pizza delivery boy. She also thought he was gay because his ear was pierced.

He was neither a pizza delivery boy nor was he gay. When he made that clear, he offered to walk her home. He dropped her off and made a date to see her the following week. After the second date he moved in with her.

"I liked her intelligence, her sense of fun, her sense of commitment, her ability to get very excited about things," says Don. "I can't imagine myself close to fifty—she can't imagine herself close to seventy. It's the difference between people who save now, to spend at some other time—and people who spend now. Age is a function of what you're thinking and how you're acting."

After living together for four years they married because Miriam became pregnant. Don had a business as a contractor and was working as an actor on the side. Miriam proposed that he take a year off so that he could take care of their daughter and continue to work on his craft.

"At first I thought she was nuts because she would be supporting me and I wouldn't be contributing my part," he says. "But the reality is that she can pull in more money than I can, and now I think it's great. For years I worked fourteen-hour days and wasn't doing what I wanted. Now I do a fair amount of day-to-day cleaning and take our daughter to school and pick her up because Miriam's work schedule is so horrendous. It's a trade-off—I take care of our daughter, but I also get to do what I want to do. We have a better life because we have more benefits. We're both committed to our daughter and our work."

♦

Other men say they are attracted to older women for the same reasons that women are often drawn to older men: They are turned on by their experience, their maturity, their charisma, and what one man called their "resonance." Age has a mystique that can galvanize younger men as well as younger women.

When Steve Harrington, a marketing executive from Illinois with dark hair, a muscular build, and an assertive manner, took a trip to the Soviet Union with his wife, he was thirty-two and his marriage was on the skids. On the tour he met Joanna, a fifty-year-old mother of six children, who shared her life in Houston with a man who was her husband in name only. Steve and Joanna began corresponding when they returned to the States and continued a long-distance romance for five years. Steve finally got divorced and persuaded Joanna to live with him.

"I felt great about the arrangement because I loved her and wanted to marry her," he says. "I can't discount the maternal part—that might have entered into it, even though I never thought about it. I wasn't hung up about the age gap, even though it was obvious that she was older—there was no mystery about it.

"She had gray—almost white—hair. She was ravishing. She also felt she had the most to lose because she felt one day she'd be sixty and I'd be forty-two and I'd decide I was with an old hag and could have zillions of younger women. That wasn't my concern. I was in love with her.

"I don't give a damn about the age or society's views. I'm not out to win popularity contests. I don't live for everyone's approval. I was with someone I loved. There's something burnished about an older woman that turns me on more in all sorts of ways than a younger woman can do."

Following Your Own Drummer

The American essayist Henry David Thoreau said that each of us has to follow the beat of our own drummer. Just as some men are turned on by women who are docile and dependent, some women are turned on by men who are pliable and compliant. Many of these women are powerful maternal figures—the mirror images of domineering men. They want to shape a relationship and they shy away from partners who are competitive or corraling. Sometimes they may be rebelling against a previous lover or a father who was dominating and repressive.

This psychological scenario, however, isn't necessarily a function of age. My grandmother, who was thirteen years younger than my grandfather, was clearly the dominating force in the family: She paid the bills, she earned the money, she taught her three boys what to do—and she was the head of the house in every conceivable way.

This dynamic can occur in almost any marriage where a woman is more assertive than a man. But nowadays a woman with this kind of temperament may find younger men more receptive to her because these men have been reared within feminist tradition.

"I was married as a child and divorced when I was thirty-five. Ultimately it broke up because I became something other than a wife. I was moving toward success in my own right, and Billy, my husband, resented it," relates Diane Wilson, a slim brunette in her mid-forties from Detroit who recently married a thirty-year-old artist. "Billy needed me as a stable wife and wanted me to complement him. He wanted me to dress well and talk well and go to luncheons and cocktail parties. I loved him very much and did many things I wouldn't do now, but I wasn't happy."

Billy was also chronically unfaithful, but he was up front about his infidelity. Diane tried to make the marriage work—partly for the sake of her son. When she was thirty-three, she decided to get her bachelor's degree in fine arts. At school she became friends with Bob, a young painter and classmate, who was tall and blond and only eighteen.

After graduating, Diane began setting up local exhibitions and developed a reputation for her curatorial skills. She also had a brief affair with a professor, and the combined events made her husband angry. "People began seeing me as Diane Wilson rather than Mrs. Wilson, and Billy developed complaints about me," she says. "I became good at something that had nothing to do with him, and it occurred to him that I could have my own life. When he found out about my affair, he called up the man and threatened to kill him. He said it was all right for him to have affairs because he said he was a 'lesser person' than I was. But he expected me to be faithful. After that it all fell apart."

Diane divorced Billy when she was thirty-five, and she set out to seduce Bob. "Getting involved with him was almost a practical, calculating thing on my part," she relates. "One night we were having a drink after class. I leaned over and gave him a kiss and said, 'I'd like to make love to you.' After a couple of weeks it happened. He was very nervous because he hadn't been with many women, and never satisfactorily. It was all very thrilling since I was the one in power and in control this time. And my experience in lovemaking was very important to him."

After her divorce they lived together for five years. Then they moved to Phoenix and married. Diane became the director of a gallery for contemporary artists and financed Bob through art school so that he could teach and continue to paint. "I never gave much thought to our age difference," she says. "Men my own age tend to bore me, because we have the same frame of reference. Bob's very quiet and his role in life is to listen and observe. His expectations are different. He doesn't want me to be less sexually aggressive and he's comfortable about me earning more money. I think he'd also be comfortable if I stayed home and he was earning money. His primary interest is making art, and we have a lot of interests in common. Even though it's possible he'd leave me for another woman, he's a very moral man, and, frankly, I might leave him instead. He has a stability in his commitments to things which is long-term and long-lasting."

That's not to say that they don't have problems. They do. But they are not caused by the age gap. Instead Diane is beginning to resent her controlling role in the relationship, even though she set it up. "Bob's unwilling and unable to deal with the practicalities of life," she says. "They don't exist for him. I pay the bills and decide where to go on vacation, and he's relieved about that because he's free to paint. But sometimes I'd like someone to take care of me. Since I'm the money maker, I'd like him to take on some of the burdens, like cooking or looking after the car, but he doesn't really know how or want to.

"I'd also like to have another child, and maybe that's crazy at my age, but Bob could care less. It might even be disastrous for him, because he'd have less time at his studio. If his career doesn't take off, that will be a problem—not the age gap. Until now it's been a good relationship because we've evolved together. All our friends are people I really like—no one ever comes over whom I don't deeply enjoy. After so many years of being accommodating, I am doing what I like."

◆

Clearly, marrying a younger man is no panacea. It can be just as problematic as marrying an older man—or a man your own age—if your needs do not mesh. What counts is knowing who you are and freeing yourself to find a partner who will satisfy you—and whom you will satisfy—no matter how old—or young—he happens to be.

In the course of researching this chapter I had lunch with an editor in her early fifties, a buxom brunette with a zesty style and seductive brown eyes. She has three grown children and divorced her husband when she was twenty-two because he wanted her to stay home. She wanted to go back to school and work. Last year she married a man in his early thirties, a tall, good-looking real-estate investor whom she met at a publishing party.

Women who find themselves in unions with younger men should take her words to heart. "I always thought, in the back of my mind, that the prince was going to come someday," she told me. "I decided he wouldn't, and my life would probably be this way from now on, and I'd have a wonderful job and friends and grandchildren, and that would be fine. I made peace with myself. Then I met Tom. When we started going out, I was so afraid someone would see us—it was like being in a closet. Now that we're married, I realize I lucked out because he's so real. He's steady. Everything I do is really important to him, and he's always there for me emotionally. His mother and I joke that when we're both in our wheelchairs, we're going to hit him with our canes. She won't be left out.

"Some younger men are attracted to older women because they're experienced and smart and attractive, but you can get burned. What I want to say is, don't limit your options because a man's fifteen years younger, or bald, or not rich enough, or not tall enough. My friends still say he's too young, but so what? If you really like him, so what? Go for it. Go for things that make you happy—and be suspicious of things that don't make you happy."

FOUR

Baby Bloomers: New Mothers Over Thirty-five

When my younger sister, Martha, was a child, she had freckles and red hair and she used to entertain our entire family with her show-biz antics and comic mimes. She also loved playing with dolls and dressing them, and when my brother, John, was born, she eagerly helped my mother take care of him. We all assumed that she would marry early and have a brood of children.

Martha married when she was thirty-seven. She gave birth to a son, Noah, four months after she turned thirty-eight. A year and a half later she gave birth to a daughter, Miranda. There's no doubt in my mind that my sister was born to be a mother. She glows every time she talks about her children, and she has thrown herself into motherhood with gusto and selfless dedication.

"I couldn't believe it when Noah was born," she says. "It was like a miracle. I was as proud as a peacock and still am. I didn't realize how much I wanted children until I had them. Now they are my work. I am totally involved with them and they are the most gratifying part of my life."

Delayed Childbearing: Fact or Fiction?

My sister's story is not uncommon. According to the National Center for Health Statistics, an unprecedented number of women are now starting families in their thirties and forties. In 1987, 16 percent of all first births were to women over the age of thirty, a fourfold increase since 1970, when only 4 percent of first births were to women over thirty (see chart G).

The most striking change has occurred among women in their late thirties, many of whom put child rearing on the back burner during the 1970s when feminism was in full gear and first-birth rates (the number of births per 1,000 women) fell to new lows: Since 1980 first-birth rates for women age thirty to thirty-four have increased by 44 percent; first-birth rates for women age thirty-five to thirty-nine have increased by *86* percent. Even first-birth rates for women age forty to forty-four have more than doubled.[1]

Roughly half of these new mothers have completed college, and a tenth are unmarried: "Women in their thirties giving birth for the first time are increasingly well-educated, and an increasing proportion of well-educated women in these age groups are giving birth,"

CHART G
Percentage of First Births by Age of Mother

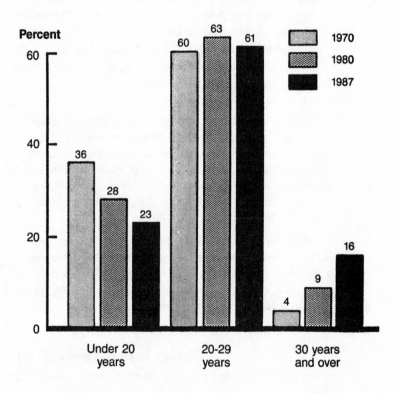

SOURCE: "TRENDS IN POSTPONED CHILDBEARING UNITED STATES, 1970
TO 87," PAPER BY STEPHANIE VENTURA, NATIONAL CENTER FOR
HEALTH STATISTICS, 1989

writes Stephanie Ventura, the author of a report on late childbearing published by NCHS.

"The only decline that has persisted since 1975 has been for women [in their twenties] who have completed college, suggesting that these women are devoting themselves to their careers and are continuing to delay marriage and childbearing"[2] (see chart H).

Clearly, starting a family in midlife is a phenomenon of the 1980s. According to Wendy Baldwin, a demographer at the Center for Population Research and coauthor of *Delayed Childbearing in the U.S.: Facts and Fictions*, this trend will continue:

> American society is changing in ways that will cause more and more women to postpone childbearing. Women now have many more life options to compete with childraising, and the contraceptive revolution has given couples much more control over the initiation of childbearing, reinforced by the availability of safe, legal abortion.

> Further, the widespread availability and use of sterilization removes the risk of unintended pregnancies after desired family size is reached. With all these changes it seems likely that delayed childbearing will remain a feature of American society.[3]

Biology Is Destiny—or Is It?

The irony is that many women have still not accepted deferred childbearing as a choice, and possibly a desirable one. When we enter our thirties and discover that our fertility, unlike our soul, is not immortal, we begin to experience all sorts of pressures and anxieties.

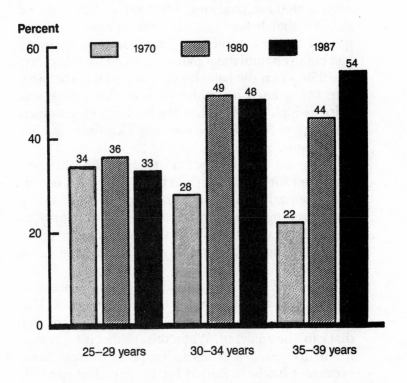

CHART H
Percentage of First Births to Mothers
Who Are College Graduates by Age

Percent

Legend: 1970 | 1980 | 1987

25–29 years: 34, 36, 33
30–34 years: 28, 49, 48
35–39 years: 22, 44, 54

SOURCE: "TRENDS IN POSTPONED CHILDBEARING UNITED STATES, 1970 TO 87," PAPER BY STEPHANIE VENTURA, NATIONAL CENTER FOR HEALTH STATISTICS, 1989

"I panicked when I reached thirty-five," says a mother who married for the first time at thirty-eight. "I felt a constant yearning to have a child because I didn't feel complete. Even though I tried to repair the void through my career and friendships, I couldn't."

A woman's biological clock is usually cited as the source of these anxieties. We tend to lose sight of the fact that before effective contraception and legalized abortion came into being, women routinely had children until menopause curtailed their fertility: In 1955, when the baby boom was peaking, the birth rate for women age thirty-five to thirty-nine was twice as high as it is today; the birth rate for women age forty to forty-four was nearly four times as high as it is now.[4]

"My great aunt had her thirteenth child when she was in her fifties and she didn't think about amniocentesis," remarked one older mother. "Now we worry about getting pregnant at thirty-six, we worry at thirty-eight, we worry at forty. We worry ourselves out of getting pregnant and enjoying the best times in our lives."

There are, however, compelling psychological factors that are also responsible for these anxieties. The urge to reproduce is an undeniable maternal instinct that can't be analyzed. When this instinct is repressed for many years, it tends to erupt with great force because it has been buried for so long. The psychologist Erich Fromm points out that for some women having children satisfies an elementary narcissistic need; for others it satisfies a craving for a singular kind of undiluted or unconditional love that is distinct from the love that exists between a mature man and woman. This craving may be particularly intense in women who are neither married nor involved in a loving relationship with a man.

But according to Fromm the most important incentive that governs almost all women is the desire for "transcendence"—the need to create and give their life meaning through the rearing of a child who bears their imprint. Men also have this need for transcendence, but because they can't bear children, they typically use work to fullfill their creative urges.[5]

Women who have been pouring their creative energies into their work may also gain transcendence in this way. But when work begins to lose its appeal as a way of personal fulfillment, as so often happens in midlife, or conversely when women gain self-confidence through their work, which may also occur in midlife, maternal yearnings that have been under cover often come to the fore.

"After women become independent and self-sufficient, their wish to be a parent often increases," states Elizabeth MacAvoy, a Manhattan therapist who has a large female caseload. "When you feel emotionally strong and complete, you are usually more equipped to give birth to a baby. When you are not hungry and feel satisfied, you can give more than when you feel empty inside and incomplete."

There are cultural factors as well that are contributing to these pressures. Many women who postponed marriage and motherhood in the 1970s were responding to the feminist norms that devalued family life. Nowadays a reaction has set in. Having babies is "in." Many women who set out to prove they could outsmart their mothers by succeeding in a male-dominated world are invested with a new sense of urgency to validate their womanhood by having children before they run out of time.

"We all thought we could have it all. We got caught up with being successful and earning money and looking for the perfect man," said a high-earning executive who had a baby when she was forty-two. "Then a friend of mine had a baby in her mid-thirties. I broke down and sobbed for four hours because she seemed to have everything and I was still muddling along in the singles scene."

We no longer idealize the single working woman and her freewheeling life-style. Instead we venerate Supermom in a pin-striped suit straddling two worlds and two wardrobes, trying precariously to juggle the demands of a crying child, the needs of a husband, the requests of a boss, and the advice of a mother-in-law.

Even Betty Friedan has now embraced mothering as a noble feminine endeavor. "To deny the part of one's being as woman that has, through the ages, been expressed in motherhood—nurturing, loving softness, and tiger strength, is to deny part of one's personhood as a woman," she writes in *The Second Stage*.[6]

Many women now view motherhood as the ultimate validation of their sexuality, the final proof that they are really females and can fulfill their biological destiny. But because these women have neither tested nor developed their maternal capacities, they often develop anxieties that young mothers don't possess.

"A lot of these women have doubts about themselves as mothers," states Joan Handler, a Manhattan therapist and older mother, in *Pregnancy Over 35*. "[Up to now] they've accented the more 'masculine' aspects of their personality. Now they wonder if they can make it as moms, if they have what it takes to function as primary caretakers. So they go through a whole crisis when they become pregnant later in life."[7]

In *The Second Stage* Betty Friedan says that feminism is and always was about choice: the "fully free" choice to have a baby or not to have a baby, to marry or not to marry, to have a baby and work—or to have a baby and not work. Many women are now asking, What choice do we realistically have?

Did we make the wrong choice when we decided, consciously or unconsciously, to defer marriage and pursue a career instead?

Will our biological clock stop before we find a husband who can be a father?

Do we need a husband to have a baby?

Do we have the ability to be competent mothers?

If we do have children, what will happen to our labors in the world, our professional identities, and our salaries?

What will happen to our children?

If we don't have a baby, will we ever really be able to fulfill our feminine destiny?

Are there other ways to nurture, give love, and bond?

Is motherhood the only answer?

◆

Because these issues are so complex and only partly within any woman's control, having a baby later in life has turned into a religious rite for scores of women, who have turned childbearing into a mission involving more sacrifice and self-abnegation than many of our mothers experienced when they shelved their career aspirations to raise us, clothe us, and bathe us with unlimited love.

"I want a baby so badly I am willing to do anything

to have one," said a married woman in her late thirties who is trying to conceive through artificial insemination. "I am doing the most embarrassing and stressful things in the world to have a child—but I am willing to do them."

Deferred Child Rearing: Plan or Accident?

The reasons that influence women not to have children in their twenties are complex. Many women who are in unhappy marriages do not want children to complicate a bad union. Other women want time to explore their options or pursue a career without the responsibilities of a husband or a child.

"I didn't want children in my twenties," says a novelist who married and bore two children after she turned thirty-five. "I wanted to lead a hippie existence and get my Ph.D. I would have been a miserable mother, because I didn't want to be tied down. I wanted to live abroad for several years and experiment."

Other women are conflicted because they sincerely want children—but their ambivalence about marriage is so overwhelming that it frustrates their maternal yearnings and sets off even more anxiety. "I always wanted children, ever since I was a little girl," said one mother who married at thirty-nine. "But I wasn't emotionally ready to settle down in my twenties, so I picked men who were unavailable. And I was so conflicted, there was a constant ache in my stomach. I was always depressed and talked about wanting children nonstop in analysis. Finally I decided that if I didn't find a husband by the age of forty, I'd adopt a child."

We don't all mature or grow at the same pace. Some

women are ready to marry and raise children in their twenties. Other women with more complicated agendas need more time. Whatever the reasons may be that cause women to postpone family life, few women who enter their thirties are immune to the anxieties that are generated by maternal yearnings, cultural pressures, and their biological clock.

All of us have to come to terms with the fact that the male shortage is real: The older we become, the fewer men there are who want to marry. Even many men who want to marry don't want families. And men who do want families don't have the same time constraints as women.

Finding a man who can be a compatible mate and a potential father is a real problem. This is compounded by the anxieties and self-doubts that also emerge at this time. Many women wind up romanticizing childbirth as the sine qua non for emotional completion, particularly if they feel unloved by men or if they are frustrated because their work doesn't fulfill them.

"Some women want to have a baby because they aren't happy with men or their life," warns Dr. MacAvoy. "They turn the project into a compulsion and use the baby as a source of love and nurturing. An infant becomes a substitute for other things that are lacking in their lives, and they tend to place too many pressures and burdens on the child. Often they end up creating too many dependencies in the child because the desire to receive nurturing is their prime motivation."

Many of us who idealized the rewards of working in our twenties now realize just how limited our visions were. We know that even the most glamorous careers can be tedious, draining, and exasperating. Idealizing childbirth can be just as self-defeating and even more dangerous. You can leave a difficult job. You cannot leave a difficult child.

Therefore, as Fromm points out, it's imperative for women to be well grounded and happy with themselves if they intend to have a child. "The narcissistic, the domineering, the possessive woman can succeed in being a 'loving' mother as long as the child is small," he warns. "Only the really loving woman, the woman who is happier giving than taking, *who is firmly rooted in her own existence*, can be a loving mother when the child is in the process of separation. . . . A woman can be a truly loving mother only if she can love, if she is able to love her husband, other children, strangers, all human beings."[8]

If you truly want to find a good husband who is a potential father, you have to be certain that the man you select will be a good partner, because raising a child imposes additional pressures on a relationship. If you rush pell-mell into a marriage with a man who is not a supportive and compatible partner, you will wind up coping with even more stresses.

Women also have the option of having a child without a husband. But if you take this route, be certain that you can cope with the financial and emotional pressures of raising a child on your own.

Whatever path you select, be clear-cut about your goals. "Lead with your head," advises one woman who married at forty and had two children. "Be practical. Know what you want. If you want a child you have to eliminate men quickly who aren't available or family-minded."

Self-confidence and good judgment are the bottom line. When your anxiety level is high—and your self-esteem is low—men who might be turned on are turned off instead.

Overcoming the Baby Blues

"I didn't panic about having a baby until I turned thirty-four—and it made me think about each new man in terms of being a marriage prospect too soon in the relationship and not let things flow naturally," says Jody Cantor, a tall, slim brunette with a deceptively easygoing manner who married and had her first baby when she was thirty-eight.

"Even though I was more independent and mature, I would feel more devastated when a relationship didn't work out than I did in my twenties. It seemed to say that my time was running out. I began feeling desperate about ever having a child."

Jody grew up in Cincinnati and went to college in Buffalo, New York. After graduating she taught elementary school. She married when she was twenty-four, mostly because her mother pushed her into it. "I don't think I ever loved him and I didn't want children because I didn't want the marriage to last," she says. "I was also scared about being on my own, but we argued so much that I finally packed my bags."

When Jody left, she was twenty-six and feminism was in full swing. She got a job as a counselor in a psychiatric hospital, dated a lot, and began rebelling against her strict background. "I didn't want to remarry—I just wanted to have a good time, so I stopped being a good girl," she relates. "I smoked pot and I had casual affairs. I never rebelled when I should have, and that retarded everything. The sooner you rebel, the sooner you find out who you are."

When she turned thirty, her enthusiasm for single

living began to wane. She decided to remarry, partly because she wanted a child. Even though she tried to be judicious about the men she dated, she wound up living with a divorced Catholic, the father of four children, who didn't want to remarry. After they broke up, she became so anxious about marrying and having a baby that she turned men off.

"I was so tense all the time that I put too much pressure on men too soon," she recalls. "I began feeling desperate, and it reached a pitch just after I turned thirty-five. I felt as though I'd met every eligible man in Buffalo I was going to meet—and they just weren't right."

When her salary was cut back by the state, she became even more depressed. She decided to return to her hometown because her family was there and she wanted a change of scene. She also did a lot of soul-searching and began to feel at peace with the baby issue. "I decided I would just live my life, and if it wasn't in the cards, it wasn't," she says. "I couldn't make it happen. So I relaxed."

In Cincinnati she got a job as a social-work supervisor and was introduced to a man by a woman she had met in a community organization. Jim was forty-nine and divorced; he was good-looking, a physicist, and considered a catch in the community—but many women had given up on him as a marriage prospect because he'd been divorced for seventeen years.

"I wanted to marry him from the beginning because everything clicked," recalls Jody. "He was exactly what I had always dreamed of, and we talked about marriage right away. We also talked about having a family. Children were important to him."

After four months of seeing each other almost every day, they had a catastrophic argument and Jim broke off the relationship. "I was devastated," says

Jody. "I didn't see him for four months. Just as I was beginning to recover, he called me. I was ready to hang up the phone and tell him to go to hell. But I felt good enough about myself to see him, and when we got together, he said he wanted to date again. He'd been under pressure because he was setting up his own business, and he couldn't handle a relationship.

"I said, 'What for? We can't go backward. Am I going to get a ring?' Usually I'm not that forthright, but I wasn't going to put up with any bull. A week later we went shopping for a ring and we married two weeks after that."

Jody got pregnant within two months and gave birth to a baby girl. Her daughter, now two, is a center in their lives. "The hard part about having kids when you're older is that they require a lot of energy," she says. "But I'm calmer now and more patient. I had a chance to do all the professional things I wanted to do. I have a sense of accomplishment. I'm home most of the time and work ten hours a week as a therapist. I don't feel I'm missing out on the rest of the world and I don't think I would have felt this way ten years ago. I don't have any ambivalence. I want her one hundred percent and feel more capable as a mother."

Clearing Up the Medical Risks

Women in their thirties often panic because they've heard so many stories about the difficulties and dangers of having a first child later in life. Many obstetricians who specialize in treating older mothers dismiss these worries: Women who are healthy and don't have a history of vaginal infections or hormonal menstrual disorders are likely to conceive and give birth to healthy children.

"A woman of any age who was healthy before the pregnancy will likely stay healthy throughout it, and deliver a healthy baby," writes Kathryn Schrotenboer-Cox, M.D., a gynecologist and author of *Pregnancy Over 35*.

"Only a woman who suffers from a chronic health problem—more common with increasing age—will be more apt to experience a difficult pregnancy. But because of the great strides made in prenatal diagnosis and care, the odds are that even she can surmount the difficulties and go on to have a perfectly normal child."[9]

David Schonholz, M.D., associate professor of gynecology and obstetrics and senior attending physician at the Mount Sinai School of Medicine in New York City, has been treating women for over thirty years. He concurs with this point of view: "The only real difficulty for women who become pregnant for the first time over thirty-five is that they have an untested reproductive system and we don't know how their uterus will respond to a pregnancy," he says. "But if a woman's never had a problem with a birth control device, such as an IUD, and if she's never had a vaginal infection of consequence, or a major surgical operation with complications, and if she has no evidence of endometriosis, she should have a normal potential for pregnancy. Birth control pills are not a factor; previous abortions or miscarriages—if they were uncomplicated and occurred within the first ten weeks of pregnancy—are also not a problem. Even if a woman is in her late forties, her main problem could be conceiving rather than carrying a healthy baby to full term. If a woman wants to have a baby, she should try to have one."

DISPELLING MYTHS

There is probably more confusion over the issue of birth defects than any other age-related issue, and because the media has given it such attention—primarily in an attempt to educate women about the realities—many women are genuinely frightened about the prospect of conceiving an abnormal fetus and going through a surgical abortion.

"When I found out I was pregnant, I was up all night crying because I was so scared I wouldn't have a healthy baby," relates a forty-two-year-old mother who had tabled the notion of getting pregnant because doctors had told her it wouldn't happen. "I didn't know what to do. It's terrifying to even think about abortion when it really pertains to you."

Statistics about the risks of conceiving abnormal fetuses are more reassuring than many of us have been led to believe: When a fetus is abnormal, the body tends to reject it spontaneously through a miscarriage. As a result only 2 percent of all babies born to women between the ages of sixteen and forty have serious birth defects; only 5 percent of babies born to women over forty have serious defects.

Of these defects Down's syndrome and, to a lesser extent, spina bifida, are age-related. According to the National Institutes of Health, the risk of conceiving a baby with Down's syndrome is about one in four hundred at the age of thirty-five; at the age of forty the odds jump to about one in one hundred. After forty the odds rise dramatically: At age forty-one they are one in eighty-two; at age forty-five, one in thirty; and at age forty-nine, one in eleven.[10]

The odds are the same for all women, whether they are new mothers or already have one or more children. They have nothing to do with heredity or even the health of the mother. Doctors are unsure of the real causes but speculate they have to do with the genetic construction of the egg, which may fluctuate or weaken over time as it is exposed to outside agents, such as radiation and toxins in the system. The increasing age of the father and paternal imprinting of the genes could also contribute.

As a result doctors advise women over thirty-five to have prenatal tests to ensure the health of their fetus. The most common one is amniocentesis, a test that extracts amniotic fluid from the uterus during the fourth month of pregnancy. Some women are now opting for a new prenatal test, chorionic villi sampling (CVS), that takes a sample of the membrane surrounding the fetal sac and can be performed as early as the eighth week of pregnancy. It can also be evaluated within two weeks.

Fertility Rites

The chief problem older women may have is conception itself. This is due to the fact that a woman is born with 400,000 eggs and usually one is emitted every month during ovulation. As these eggs age, it is harder for them to be fertilized because they are weaker. Therefore an older woman may have to have intercourse through more ovulation cycles than a younger woman before her egg connects with a sperm. Even so, many experts contend that the concern over delayed conception is overblown. A recent study of 792 pregnancies shows that the median time for conception for women age fifteen to twenty-five is two months; for women age thirty-five to forty-four the median time is only 3.8 months.[11]

Since the speed at which you conceive is directly related to the number of efforts you make—experts suggest coitus three or four times during the week that ovulation is occurring—the reasons obstructing speedy pregnancies may be related to the infrequency of intercourse rather than the age of a woman.

On the other hand older women are more prone to conditions that often interfere with fertility: The most common are endometriosis, an accumulation of tissue that becomes attached to pelvic organs and can block the passage of eggs; sexually transmitted genital infections, such as chlamydia and mycoplasma, which tend to occur more frequently in women who have had a wide variety of sexual partners; pelvic inflammatory disease (PID); and luteal-phase defect, a condition in which a small hormone-producing cyst in the ovary that supports early pregnancy doesn't function properly. Fortunately most of these conditions can be detected easily—and cured. New advances in test-tube fertilization may also help women who don't respond to conventional fertility drugs.

Physicians point out that a man should be tested as well: According to a cover story in *Time* magazine (November 1984), about 40 percent of diagnosable cases of infertility can be attributed to the man and 20 percent to both partners.[12]

MISCARRIAGES: MIND OVER MATTER?

Many older women are deterred by grim stories about women who miscarry when they conceive later in life. In 1986 the University of Wisconsin Medical School compiled studies of miscarriage rates and set up estimated ranges of 7.2 to 15 percent for women age twenty to twenty-nine, 13.5 to 20.5 percent for those thirty to thirty-nine, and 21 to 46.1 percent for women forty and older.[13]

Doctors speculate that the increase is due to the fact

that as a woman ages, she's more prone to conceiving a fetus with genetic abnormalities, which the body tends to abort spontaneously. Another common cause is a poor union of an egg and a sperm, which can happen more often in an older woman because her egg—and her partner's sperm—are older and therefore weaker.

Even so, doctors contend there's little if any relationship between miscarriages and healthy pregnancies. "Many women have a miscarriage and then a baby, or a baby and then a miscarriage, or two miscarriages and a baby," maintains Dr. Schonholz. "There's no cause and effect."

CHILDBIRTH

There's a widespread belief that it's more difficult for a woman in her late thirties—or forties—to go through the experience of childbirth than a woman who has already borne children. Many physicians reject this notion. "The problems in a mother who carries a baby are related to weight gain, hypertension, underlying cardiac problems, diabetes, and vascular changes—but these can occur in all women, irrespective of previous pregnancies," says Dr. Schonholz.

There's also a growing concern about the increasing tendency for doctors to perform cesarean sections on older mothers, particularly if it's a woman's first child. Currently one out of every four mothers over thirty-five has a surgical delivery. Strictly speaking, a C-section is called for when a baby is in the wrong position to come out normally, or when the mother's uterus is too narrow to facilitate a natural passage. When older women suffer from health problems that can affect the baby, doctors often opt for a cesarian birth to ensure the health of the mother and the child.

Some older mothers may also experience dystocia —a long and painful labor that does not progress normally because the uterus is older and the uterine muscles are therefore weaker and less effective in making the contractions needed to push out the baby vaginally.

If a woman is not a real candidate for any of these conditions, she is likely to have an easy pregnancy and natural childbirth. "The same hormones that soften the uterus of a twenty-year-old soften the uterus of a forty-year-old," says Dr. Schonholz. "What you're dealing with many times is a great anxiety at giving birth for the first time, and there's a relationship between anxiety and the progression of labor—even though there's no study on how women might have reacted if they'd been given medication to assuage the anxiety."

The increasing incidence of cesarian births is partly a reaction to this anxiety, which both the doctor and the patient feel. "An older mother is often perceived as a problem, and no one wants to risk an unsafe birth," argues Dr. Schonholz. "Instead of following the heartbeat of the child, in relation to labor contractions and acidosis, a doctor opts for a cesarian."

There is a great deal of lively debate about the wisdom—and ethics—of performing cesarian sections when the position of the baby does not absolutely warrant it. Women who are concerned about the prospect are usually advised to take up the issue ahead of time with their physician, instead of depending upon their husband to make the decision in the delivery room. They may also ask a physician to look into— or undertake—some of the new procedures that are being devised for intralabor testing and the management of labor.

The Mommy Track—or Mommy Trap?

In 1980, 50 percent of the women over thirty who gave birth to a first child were working in a professional job; more than a third were sales, clerical, or service workers, and a minimal 4 percent were working in other types of jobs. Only 9 percent were unemployed at the time of birth.[14]

Working mothers are a reality today, and even if a woman has a baby for all the right reasons—and with the right partner—many don't fully appreciate the kinds of stresses that can develop when they actually have a child. Some women decide to drop out of their career and stay home with their infant full-time. But this is a luxury that few women can afford.

In 1950, only 12 percent of women with children under six years of age were working. In 1984, 52 percent of women with children under the age of six were working. For mothers of school-age children, age six to seventeen, the increase was from 28 percent who worked in 1950 to 65 percent who were working in 1984.[15]

Juggling a career and a family is no longer an option, but a necessity for many women who need a second income to keep their child clothed and fed. Yet women are still laboring under traditional constraints that double their burden. A recent book, *The Second Shift*, shows that in most traditional marriages women are expected to do most of the child-rearing and household chores, even if they are working full-time.[16]

Two years ago Felice N. Schwartz, the founder and president of Catalyst, an advisory group on women's leadership, wrote a controversial article, "The

Mommy Track," that provoked debate because she argued that mothers working in corporations should be groomed for jobs that are less high-pressured and demanding than those set up for high-ranking executives who often have to work killing hours.[17]

In fact some corporations are now setting up innovative ways of keeping mothers happy and on the job as well: Extended leaves of absence, flexible scheduling, on-site day-care centers, and alternative career tracks are just some of the methods that various companies are instituting.

But this is still a sticky point among working moms, some of whom resent the fact that they have to soft-peddle their careers while they raise their children. Those with enough money can hire full-time nannies, who will take care of their child while they work full days. Others have to come to terms with the fact that something has to give.

"I knew I wanted children at some point down the road and imagined I would continue in my career, which isn't the way things worked out," says Suzanne Turner, a former bank executive who had twins in her mid-thirties. "When I returned to work after five months at home, I always felt I was in the wrong place at the wrong time. If I was working, I wanted to be home, and if I was home, I wanted to be working. I couldn't work at the same pace—and I didn't want a slower and dumber job. I was about to do a bad job at both, and since I would rather do one thing and succeed at it than do a mediocre job at a lot of things, I decided to quit. I also didn't want to hand over the raising of my children to someone else."

After several months she started her own business importing children's clothing from Brazil, an enterprise she operated from her home. "I liked my kids a lot," she says. "They're fun and I wanted to be with them. Women really do have to make a choice—you can't do it all—you wind up doing a crummy job at one. When I took all this into account, I realized there were alternatives within my own life-style."

Other women who are psychologically—and financially—prepared to put their careers on the back burner while they raise their children are confounded when other pressures develop: They discover they're not prepared to be full-time moms. This is particularly true of career women who are perfectionists. They know how to get a job done and they are also used to being in control of their lives. They are skilled at making schedules, solving crises, and making sure that everything works.

But babies don't respond well to regimentation. They don't eat on time, they cry at odd hours, and they throw toys on the floor. As Linda Gunsberg points out in an article on older mothers that appeared in *Lear's* magazine, many women who defer child rearing take it more seriously than women who have children earlier in life.[18]

"Five weeks after Dena was born, I was a wreck," explains Diane Talbot, a high-earning sales executive who had her first baby at forty. "She cried all the time, and I didn't know why, and it drove me crazy. I didn't know how to make her stop—and I didn't know what to do with my time.

"Maybe if I'd had children earlier in life, it would have been easier to adapt, but I'd been working for fourteen years and it was hard for me. I'm used to being in charge and having things run on a schedule.

"I went back to work nine weeks after she was born because I was so unhappy at home. Now tears come into my eyes whenever I think of my daughter, and I think she's an unbelievable child. If I were younger, I'd have three more. I love coming home at night, I love long weekends—but I look forward to going back to work."

The Psychological Rewards of Working

Diane's story is not unusual: Many professional women find they have the same kind of intolerance for being with children full-time that many men express. It's not that these women lack nurturing qualities or the ability to be good mothers. But they are used to the stimulation and orderly domain of the working world, and they still invest a lot of their ego in their careers, particularly if they have been successful.

"A lot of my identity is tied up in my profession," says Pat Kinder, the chairman of a speech therapy department in a large urban hospital who had two children in her forties. She was able to arrange a four-day work schedule when both babies were born.

"If I had just been a line employee, I might not have gone back. But I had an established career. I have good day hours and vacations, and I can often call my own shots. My department runs beautifully without me, or with me even if I'm tired.

"Even though I love my days with my children, if I had to do it seven days, it wouldn't be enough to satisfy me. They're wonderful and terrific, and marrying my husband and having them was probably the best thing I ever did, but there's more to life. There's more to your brain. I'm not a homemaker; I never bake. And if you wrap your whole life around your kids and you're not having a large family, what do you do when they go to school?"

Clearly Pat is fortunate because she is free to ar-

range her own schedule and take time off when it's
needed; her husband is extremely involved with the
children and really pitches in; she has many friends
who are older mothers; and she has a lot of energy
and enthusiasm that carry her through tough moments. She's even-keeled, well-organized, and able to
handle a lot.

Many other women are not able to set up flexible
schedules in their jobs because they work in more rigid
structures. For them the answer is either developing
a home-based business, working part-time as a consultant in their field, or taking a low-pressure job.
Even women who are not stars in their field say they
need the space and stimulation of an independent
work life.

"I love my children and would kill for them, but I
can't stay home for them," says Eileen Bach, a forty-
four-year-old mother and pension administrator in
Fort Lauderdale, who now takes care of five step-
children and two children of her own.

When Eileen was thirty-nine, she moved to Florida
from New York City at the request of a co-worker in
her office, who wanted Eileen to work for him. At the
time she was recovering from a bad love affair and
decided a change would be good for her. Soon after
she arrived, Bob—her co-worker and new boss—
found himself in the midst of a divorce he didn't want.
He had five children ranging in age from two to
eleven, and his wife said she wanted a divorce because
she was having an affair with another man. Bob
leaned on Eileen for support and friendship; a year
later he proposed and she accepted. A week before
their wedding Bob's wife deposited all five children
at their home. "I was so overwhelmed that I put off
the wedding for a while," says Eileen. "I would go to
the bathroom just to get some quiet. We all lived to-

gether for a month, and gradually I began to like the kids. When we decided to get married, all of us got married and they called me Mommy right away.

"Then I decided since I was already taking care of his children, why not have one of my own? You can't possibly love someone else's children as much as your own. When I was forty-two, I decided to have a second child so the first one wouldn't be alone."

After Eileen put her second child in preschool, she couldn't stand being at home anymore and decided to get a full-time job. "I work to get out of the house," she says. "When I had two babies, I was really tied down and I found myself in the house a lot and I didn't like it. At first I thought I would go crazy—home to me is a place to be alone."

They now live in a six-bedroom house, and everyone pitches in: Bob makes lunch for the children and lays out their clothes; Eileen dresses her youngest child before she goes to work; the older siblings dress themselves and make their beds before Eileen leaves for her job.

The children all get home at different times in the afternoon and are old enough to take care of themselves. Eileen picks up her youngest child at preschool after she leaves her job. When she gets home, she makes dinner, bathes the youngest children, gets into her pajamas, and goes to bed early.

"I didn't marry to have children," she says. "I married Bob because he was my best friend. But basically they are good kids and I never even thought of having my own until I had his. Bob is very good to us—he works hard for us, he cleans the house, he's very caring, and he's always reliable. I never felt so healthy and fulfilled as when I was pregnant. But I also need to work."

Eileen's story is unusual in many ways. After all

how many women nowadays have seven children underfoot and work full-time as well? What it highlights is that even women with strong maternal abilities don't take to full-time motherhood the way a duck takes to water. Yet these women are often more effective parents than younger women who are still restless and unformed.

A study done in 1982 by Steven Frankel, a psychiatrist at the University of California Medical Center in San Francisco, and Myra Wise, a psychiatrist at Children's Hospital there, compared women who had babies after the age of thirty with women who had babies before thirty. They found that older mothers tended to be "more accepting and less conflicted in the parenting role" and showed "strengths which were concomitant with their level of maturity and which seemed generally advantageous for their children's development."[19]

Even though studies such as this don't analyze the extent to which work may contribute to this state of well-being, my own research indicates that most women need a balance. The fact that they're no longer striving to make it in their career erases many of the tensions that younger mothers may feel—but they still need the space and sense of identity that work provides.

"I really like my work, and it's a lot easier than taking care of a child," says a forty-one-year-old manager and new mother. "You can't reason with an infant. I'm a high-energy person, and babies are slow. I prefer quality time with her instead. She has my full attention on weekends—I slow down my pace and am free to enjoy her fully. I'm a better parent this way because I'm doing what I want to do in both worlds."

Clearly women who postpone child rearing have restricted choices: We *are* constrained by biology; we *are* restricted by corporate structures; we may be constrained by traditional husbands who don't want to share child rearing and household chores. We are all constrained by individual preferences, life-styles, needs, and desires. But we do not have to succumb to despair or make rash decisions in an effort to beat the baby clock.

Many of us have benefited from our life experience. We have the choice to be happy with ourselves and what we've accomplished. If you're not happy with yourself when you set out to have a baby, it's not likely you'll be happy when you have one. Babies provide a unique nurturing experience, but child rearing also entails stresses and demands that can be enormously draining. That is why you have to know what to expect if you plan to have a baby. The issue is not simply finding a husband who will be a father. The issue is raising a child in a home where there's real love, concern, and stability.

For many women, developing bonds with others can be as deeply satisfying a way of expressing their nurturing selves. When we identify our options and take stock of who we are and what will make us happy, we will be more likely to get what we want—and need.

Miracle Brides: Saying "I Do" Over Forty

I grew up in the era when marrying early was the rule and it was rare for women to have careers. When I graduated from Barnard College in the early 1960s, our president, Millicent MacIntosh—a feminist who married in her thirties and had five children by the age of forty—encouraged us to prepare for dual roles as wives and workers. Only a handful of my classmates had the self-confidence and drive to attempt both. Many thought we had to make a choice: Either we could raise a family and work part-time in low-paying fields or we could pursue rigorous careers and reject marriage.

Most of my classmates opted for full-time motherhood and shelved their career ambitions until their mid-thirties, when many of them entered professional

schools. I took a difficult path. I had a fierce desire
to get my Ph.D. in English literature, teach in a university, and live abroad. When marriage-minded suitors appeared on the scene, I rejected them because I
was not ready to renounce my independence and
modify my ambitions.

In my mid-twenties I accepted a teaching position
at Queens College in New York City. I was one of the
few women in my department and the youngest faculty member. It was the late '60s, and feminism was
beginning to take root. I easily found friends who
were my mirror images: We were all more intent on
exploring life than on marrying or having children.
So we diligently pursued our goals, oblivious to the
notion that either age or biology would ever cause us
to revise our dreams.

Euphoria carried us along as we had sexual adven-
tures, earned money, and found out that we could
make it on our own. But when we entered our forties,
our own midlife changes were reinforced by social
changes as the communal values of the We decade
began to usurp the self-obsessed values of the Me
decade. We began having serious misgivings about
our single status. We discussed the subject with therapists and talked about it endlessly on the telephone
and in women's groups. Were we single because we
were too successful—or were we successful because
we were single? Were we rejecting marriageable
men—or were marriage-minded men rejecting us?

In fact these questions are tough to answer. His-
torically, educated women have been less likely to
marry than women who have not been to college. One
study shows that almost 30 percent of the women who
graduated from a prestigious woman's college between 1911 and 1915 never married.[1] Nowadays, the
widespread entry of women into colleges and profes-

sional schools has changed this pattern dramatically. College-educated women still marry later than women who have not completed college, but according to Jeanne Moorman, college-educated women in their twenties and early thirties are *more* likely to marry at some point than their peers who have not completed college. (A thirty-year-old single woman, for example, with *five* years or more of college has a *greater* chance of marrying than a thirty-year-old single woman with four years of college or a high school degree.) Even college-educated women in their late thirties are just as likely to marry as women who are only high school graduates.

In contrast, marriage probabilities for single, highly educated women over forty are still not as great as they are for women who haven't completed college, but the differences are not significant. (Roughly 20 percent of single college-educated women age forty to forty-four are expected to marry, compared with about 24 percent of women age forty to forty-four who have only high school degrees.)[2]

One reason for the disparity is conditioning: Many men and women raised in prefeminist times still abide by the norm that a man should be more educated and successful than his spouse. As a result, women who want to marry "up" have restricted options, while men who want to marry "down" have wide choices.

But conditioning is not the only reason for this pattern, and it may not be the primary one. Many highly educated women have high-paying jobs and therefore they don't have the same financial pressures as other women to find husbands who will support them. They are freer to be selective and to lead fulfilling lives on their own.

Many, in fact, are single by choice. But because there is still such a strong societal bias equating the mere ability to get married with mental health, women who have never married are often subject to self-doubts and anxieties that don't trouble women who were once married. Even some committed feminists are defensive about their never-married status. "I'm single but I tell everyone I'm divorced so they won't think I'm a freak," commented a feminist in her forties at a NOW convention some years back.

Psychology and the Single Woman

The source of these anxieties is cultural as well as psychological. Throughout Western civilization women who never married were stigmatized and often caricatured in literature as sexless and barren old maids. In the early 1900s women had almost no career options and little status. Respectable women who didn't marry made their way as governesses, domestics, and nurses. They were members of a silent minority, who were seen but not heard, tolerated but not revered. They were often branded *spinsters*—a term that originated in preindustrial England to describe unmarried women who lived at home and earned their keep spinning wool.

Eventually the term *spinster* became a catchall for any unmarried woman—the counterpart of *bachelor* —and it developed perjorative connotations, because marriage in those years was considered the only desirable way of life for women. Bachelors were also viewed with skepticism, but they were socially desirable and could rise to the top in whatever profession they selected. Many were looked upon as Mama's boys; others were viewed as bon vivants.

Even when women began working outside the

home in the early twentieth century, most who didn't marry were restricted to jobs as teachers, nurses, librarians, sales clerks, and secretaries. Only rare women with unusual drive and talent—such as the novelist Edith Wharton, the labor agitator Emma Goldman, and M. Carey Thomas, the first president of Bryn Mawr—had the courage to defy convention and become well-known figures in their own right.

When Sigmund Freud began his seminal work on human behavior in the late nineteenth and early twentieth centuries, he lent these societal attitudes scientific weight. He asserted that girls as well as boys had a masculine orientation until puberty, at which point a girl's sexual glands began to function. If she developed normally, she would complete her sexual destiny by marrying and having children. According to Freud, a woman who never married remained single not out of conscious choice, but because she was inhibited by infantile neurotic conflicts.[3]

Nowadays many critics maintain that Freud's view of female development is hostile and just plain wrong. Yet some people still insist that a woman's sexual normalcy is predicated on her ability to marry and bear children. (If she is divorced, she may have made a mistake, but at least she isn't unnatural.) Even modern therapists who have modified Freud's basic views maintain that women who remain single into their forties are inhibited by unconscious neurotic conflicts stemming from faulty parenting. "Often you find a breakdown in parental relationships," says Dr. Diane Kirschner. "If your mother wasn't prized in the family or if she doesn't prize you, you can grow up feeling devalued. If you're treated like a boy by your father, you may not develop a secure sense of feminine identity."

Other women may be so dominated by their parents

that they never develop the ability to break away and form independent relationships with men. "There's often an unconscious wish on the part of the parents not to let the child go," says Dr. Kirschner. "A woman may form a reverse parental relationship—caring for her parents, particularly her mother, emotionally and even financially—and she may experience anxiety and guilt in binding heterosexual relationships, because she is terrified of leaving her parents and losing their love."

Other therapists disagree. They maintain that even if a woman was hampered by neurotic conflicts about bonding in her twenties, she has possibly resolved these issues by her mid-thirties, particularly if she has attained success in her career. As she nears her forties, the shortage of men induces other psychological traumas that have little to do with initial childhood conflicts.

"Clinically I see no difference between my women patients who married and those who did not," states Dr. Janice Lieberman. "There are married women who fear intimacy and married women who have terrible relationships with their mothers. Sometimes it's the healthier woman who didn't marry and compromise. But society refuses to give credence to the fact that there truly exists a shortage of men capable of committed relationships. It's easier to blame women —who have traditionally carried the blame for society's ills—for failing to develop sound relationships than to acknowledge this painful reality."

Indeed the factors that influence women to remain single into their forties are complex. They are usually a mix of internal and external pressures, and even therapists who treat these women can't pinpoint all the reasons.

It's just as difficult to isolate the specific factors that

influence women to either change their mind-set or find husbands after many years of single living. In the course of researching this chapter, I found that the most common denominator was a growing sense of self-esteem and the development of new goals. Some women were clearly caught up in neurotic patterns, which they managed to transcend only when they developed their self-confidence. Many others experienced a midlife crisis similar to that which seizes hard-driving men, and it usually occurred when they reached a plateau in their careers.

Shifting Priorities

The psychologist Carl G. Jung was the first to propose that the human personality is not static—as Freud maintained—but evolutionary, and that it changes over time. He said that between thirty-five and forty the psyche goes through changes that trigger new goals and fantasies. Many men experience a midlife crisis when they realize that success and power are no longer personally fulfilling. Some reach a pinnacle and realize that they can't go farther; others realize that they will never attain what they set out to do. In either case disillusionment sets in, and men often switch gears and look for activities that are more nurturing.

The psychologist Erik Erikson, who also believes that the psyche progresses in a series of phases, called this process *generativity*—a movement away from self-absorption and toward involvement with others.[4]

Gail Sheehy, who popularized these theories in *Passages*, points out that men who have set great store by their careers may take on voluntary charitable work, set up career tracks that are more people-oriented, or become mentors to youngsters. "Many men in their forties do experience a major shift of emphasis away from pouring their energies into their own advancement," she writes. "They begin taking pleasure in teaching other people or correcting social injustices."[5]

Sheehy also describes the midlife crisis experienced by women. But since she did her research in the early 1970s, when feminism was still new and most mature women were full-time caretakers and mothers, she noted an opposite shift: Women who spent their twenties and thirties developing their nurturing capacities began to feel yearnings in midlife to express their assertive nature and develop an identity in the working world. Some women, for example, started careers; others studied for advanced degrees.

She couldn't observe the phenomenon that is occurring today among baby-boom women who have deferred marriage to pursue careers: When women repress the maternal or nurturing sides of their personalities in order to compete with men, they go through the same kind of generative process that men do. But when this change occurs in women, it explodes with even more force. Women experience this crisis not only as a disillusionment with the rewards of success but also as an urgent need to validate their sexuality and cultivate their dormant feminine qualities.

"At forty a midlife transition occurs because the life structure cannot continue unchanged," says Daniel Levinson, who is now completing a book on the stages of a woman's life. "If a woman has built her life around her career, she has to deal more directly with the absence of a family and the meaning of her work and its limitations. Often she feels cheated and begins to question her identity as a female. Matrimony and motherhood become major issues."

Many seek a primary relationship with a man who gives them a chance to be nurturing—and nurtured. Often the change is triggered by a woman's biological clock and manifests itself in a strong desire to have children. Other women soft-peddle their careers and take on roles that are more people-oriented.

In 1970 Margaret Hennig studied the life cycles of high-achieving women for her doctoral dissertation at Harvard Business School. Later expanded and published as *The Managerial Woman,* it still stands as one of the most incisive studies on the changes that career women experience.[6] She traced the lives of twenty-five women who had attained top corporate positions as vice presidents or presidents. All of these women were firstborn children. They were inspired to succeed by their fathers who developed a good rapport with them and taught them to think independantly and embrace tasks that entailed risk. Their mothers were traditional homemakers and had less influence on their development. In their twenties these women rejected marriage to pursue their ambitions. When they reached thirty-five, they all took time off from their jobs for a year or two. They continued to work, but with less zeal, and focused instead on their social lives. Half the group married; the other half took less-pressured jobs and became more involved in mentoring or nurturing activities.

Hennig also did a control study with middle-management women and found that all of them had been treated like boys by their fathers. They grew up with confused notions of their own sexuality and related to men as buddies rather than romantic partners. They never managed to integrate their masculine and feminine selves. Even though they wanted to marry, they never did. In their fifties, they seemed bitter, lonely, and frustrated.

This study shows that many women who rise to the top in a male-dominated field go through the same passage that men often experience. More important, it suggests that a woman's self-image and her sexuality are at the core of her ability to attract men and be receptive to them. When a career is only masking a woman's insecurities as a female, she may not be able to make the transition to married life, even though she may profess a desire to do so.

Many of the women I interviewed went through the same process Hennig described in her study of high achievers. When they attained a certain level of success in their work, they experienced the acute sense of loss that often occurs when a primary goal is achieved. This was followed by what some women described as a "reawakening"—a personal epiphany —that steered them toward a new course that involved bonding with a nurturing mate, marrying, and, in some cases, having children.

Dreaming the Wrong Dream

"When I was in my twenties, I equated marriage with a sense of dying," says Joanne Stein, a slim public relations executive with curly brown hair, who married for the first time when she was forty-three. "I wanted to travel and live a New York City life and build a career and make money. I did everything I wanted, and then I got to the point where I began feeling lonely inside and wanted a man who was caring and 'there.' "

Joanne grew up in a small town in Pennsylvania. Her father died before she was born, and her mother never remarried or even dated. "I never saw a real relationship in my home," she says. "I never saw the joy part. I thought I would lose too much freedom if I married and had children. I didn't want the give-and-take. In college I used to feel isolated from my sorority sisters who all wanted to get married right away."

After she graduated, Joanne moved to New York City and got a job in book publishing that she still describes as a fantasy come true. "It opened up a whole new vista," she says. "I met fabulous people; I liked working, and it all seemed more wonderful than being married and raising kids."

When she was twenty-six, she met a man in his late thirties and lived with him for a year. But when he proposed, she turned him down. "He wanted me to renovate a kitchen, and I thought, Why should I do that? I liked working and didn't like housekeeping. I didn't have deep yearnings for children."

At thirty Joanne got a job with a large public relations firm, handling the publicity for celebrities and movie stars. She went to private screenings and swank parties. Money was never an issue; she bought what she wanted.

She was also outgoing and dated a lot, but she tended to select men who were superficially exciting. When she went to press parties, she would "work a room" and meet any man she wanted to. "I was a smiler," she says, "and men liked that. I'd simply go up to them and say, 'Hello,' or 'I like your shirt.' "

She had two long-term romances during those years, but neither worked out. When she turned thirty-five, her dream began to pall. "My career was losing its luster," she says. "It didn't have the appeal and energy it had when I was building it up. The aggravation began to increase—working with celebrities requires tremendous patience—and when I had to take a Valium one day, I realized it wasn't worth it."

She began to feel an intense emptiness inside, but she still wasn't ready, at the deepest level, to marry. "I was still critical of men who weren't jazzy on the surface," she says. "And my life was full. I had terrific friends; I was always busy. But loneliness began gnawing at me."

The turning point came when she reached forty-one. Her mother was stricken with Alzheimer's disease, and it caused Joanne to rethink her goals. "I stopped dating the man I'd been seeing because he didn't want to deal with my problems—on a deeper level he wasn't really my friend and he wasn't even nice," she recalls. "I realized I was overlooking the deeper layers in my life and needed a man who was caring and reliable."

After she broke up with her boyfriend, she became very depressed and, on a whim, she signed up with a Jewish dating service that charged only thirty-five dollars.

Several weeks later she received a call from a forty-eight-year-old stockbroker. Jack was tall and balding, with a paunch. He was successful in his field, but not as slick as the men she was used to dating. He was also an observant Jew and extremely family-minded. He took care of his father after his mother died, and when his father died, he was introduced to a lot of women but he didn't like any of them. So he signed up with the dating service. They gave him Joanne's name and he called her in June.

"I wasn't even sure of his last name when I accepted the date," says Joanne. "And when Jack said he was kosher, I thought, Cross him off the list. But I was lonely and depressed and wanted to get into things again."

Jack kept asking her out, and she kept on seeing him. As she puts it, she wasn't "flying" after a date, but she always had a good time. Jack sensed her indifference. "He didn't know if I really liked him until I asked him to go to the movies with me," she admits now. "He crept into my heart. I could see that he was a sweet, good man who was really very happy and that he was different from anyone else I knew. He always made me laugh."

In late August Jack took her to Florida for a vacation. When they returned, they began seeing each other several times a week. A year later they moved in together, and he asked her to marry him soon after. "He turned out to be my dream man—before we met I was dreaming the wrong dream. There are a lot of men to marry if you're receptive and willing to adjust. Jack and I have our differences, but we're really well suited. When I met him, I was ready inside."

Letting Go

Most of my peers and I were conditioned to marry men who would take care of us in every way. My own father was a self-educated corporation president, a superior athlete, a community leader, a devoted family man, and a teetotaler. I nicknamed him "EV" for "Eminent Victorian."

I used to measure all my dates against him, and they inevitably fell short. If they were very successful and ambitious, they often turned out to be womanizers, impotent, or simply too self-involved to carry on a relationship. And if they didn't tower over me professionally, I couldn't respect them.

Like many other women I've had to readjust the criteria I've used to size up good men. As Germaine Greer stated in *The Female Eunuch*, it might be healthy egotism—and completely natural—for women to select men who are successful and superior to them, if it weren't for the fact that we too often define superiority in ways that are either trivial or commercial.[7]

One problem for many career women is that if you continue to look for men who are more successful than you are, the slimmer your choices will be. The more basic problem involves setting up professional success as a sine qua non for good mates. Many men who are extremely successful may be reliable, responsive, affectionate, and considerate. Many other high-achieving men can be egotistical, narcissistic, or too threatened by successful women to be good partners—and women who marry them often have to spend most of their time catering to their needs. Conversely many men who are moderately successful may be affectionate, sensitive, responsible, and genuinely interesting. Success in the professional sphere, in short, cannot be the bottom line if you are looking for a man who can be a nurturing partner.

"There is a shortage of men, but my sense is that women who complain about this need men who are taller than them in every way," says therapist Robin Ashman. "And there aren't enough men who are superior in every way. If you're short and limited yourself, it isn't hard to find someone taller and bigger, but if you're going to grow and develop, you're going to need more of an equal partner. Many women want a nurturing man who is also aggressive, but nurturing men aren't usually aggressive men. And if you're aggressive yourself, you might not get along with an aggressive man—but you can't be contemptuous of him for not being aggressive. The time when successful women will find more men available to them is when they realize they don't need someone who's more successful than they are—they need a man who's happy in his work. You have to figure out what you want and tolerate the disappointments that may ensue when you realize a man is a person and not a superhero."

The Three-Piece-Suit Syndrome

"After I turned thirty-five, I began feeling there was no one out there for me. So I began shopping for a man," says Nancy Taylor, a black woman with a pleasant face, bobbed hair, a slightly buxom build, and a soft-spoken but firm manner.

Black professional women are more restricted than white women when it comes to finding suitable partners. "There are more white men out there for white women than black men for black women," says Nancy, who lives in Chicago. "My friends get out; they know who's there. The problem is they don't have as many structured ways to meet. There aren't many singles organizations or Personals ads just for blacks."

Nancy grew up on a farm in Wisconsin, the youngest of six children. Her mother died when she was nine. Her father remarried, had three more children and moved to Beloit, where he became a factory worker. "It was tough," she says. "All of us worked and we bought our clothes with the money we earned from our jobs. My goal was to go to college so that I could have a career and earn enough money to afford the things I wanted. I didn't want to marry until some-time after I turned forty."

After graduating from the University of Wisconsin, Nancy moved to Chicago and got a job as a city plan-ner, eventually working with community groups and hospitals to set up health-care plans. "I would spend long hours at work and when I got home, I would always set the table and fix a proper meal," she says. "I would even buy special clothes just to wear around the house, because I felt that I deserved it. I always treated myself well. I wasn't looking to marry and I always had friends to go out with to dinner or for a drink or a play."

When Nancy turned thirty-five, her confidence be-gan to ebb, and she started to panic about finding a husband. Like many of her peers, she wanted a man who was her professional equal. "My career was doing well, and I had acquired material things," she says, "but it became frustrating to date because the men who economically met the criteria I had in mind were jerks. They were cocky and because they were so much in demand, they felt they could treat women any way they wanted."

Finally she stopped worrying about finding a man to marry. Instead she decided to expand her horizons and date men who would be good company. "I re-alized you can't find the perfect man and I was putting too many restrictions on myself," she explains.

"I dated a lot of different men—I met some of them walking down the street: Men would say, 'Hi, babe,' and I'd say, 'Hi.' Most women wouldn't talk to them, so they would be shocked. By the time I told them about myself, we would wind up having lunch or din-ner. I became more open—and honest—about what I wanted. If you're looking for companionship, it doesn't matter if a man wears a three-piece suit and carries a briefcase. What's wrong if a man works with his hands? He might also have creative interests. I dated a construction worker and a man who worked on an assembly line. It was enlightening to me because I found they had a lot of good basic values. I just wanted a man who was down-to-earth and who would make me laugh."

One day after she turned forty, she went into the garage of her apartment building to collect her car. There she met a neighbor—a black man dressed in work clothes, who was getting his bicycle. "We chatted, and then he rode over to the park on his bike where I was doing some sketching and we arranged our first date," she recalls. "Then we began seeing each other. He would cook and invite me to dinner, and I would invite him over when I entertained. It was easy to get to know each other and build a relationship quickly. He was divorced and told me right up front, 'I'm broke and will be broke for about four years, since I have two sons in college.'

"For four months I didn't even know what he did for a living. He was always wearing grubby clothes, and I thought he was a car mechanic. But I didn't care, because I wasn't looking for anything."

Andrew, it turned out, was a forty-six-year-old sales manager who worked for an automotive firm, and he wore work clothes because he had to call on garage owners to sell products. I met him in Chicago, and he's a tall, good-looking man with a beard, who exudes macho charm and vitality. He had married in his early twenties and divorced his wife because she was an alcoholic. He spent the next sixteen years trying to win custody of his sons and taking care of them on weekends and evenings.

A year after Andrew met Nancy, she moved to New Jersey because she got a better job offer. They stayed in touch, and when she moved back to Chicago a year later, they decided to live together. Three months later, on New Year's Eve, he opened a bottle of champagne and popped the question. They married the following fall.

"It was easy getting along with Andrew," she says. "He didn't have hang-ups talking about what he had or didn't have. He has a good sense of humor, and we could talk about stupid things and laugh. I was impressed because he really cared about his sons— he had a great sense of responsibility and reminded me of my father. His values are in place, and you don't find a lot of men with the right sense of values."

◆

When you finally see that your idealized vision of a spouse may be self-limiting, that marrying a senior vice president won't necessarily make you feel loved, happy, and secure, you can move forward and look for a man who will be emotionally supportive and responsive. Opening up to a variety of men and being willing to explore what they have to offer—and what you have to offer them—will enhance your chances of finding exactly what you want.

The Case for Identity

In *The Art of Loving* Erich Fromm maintains that healthy unions can only develop when each person has a clear and secure sense of his or her own value. "Mature love," he states, "is a union under the condition of preserving one's integrity, one's individuality." It involves "a state of intensity, awakeness, enhanced vitality, which can only be the result of a productive and active orientation in many other spheres of life."[8]

Children who aren't encouraged to develop autonomy in their teens often marry soon after college because they can't tolerate living on their own. Frequently they choose spouses who are similarly dependent. Stanton Peele, a psychologist who has taught at Harvard and Columbia, is the author of *Love and Addiction*, a study about why people form self-destructive relationships.[9] He maintains that people with overwhelming dependency needs are often raised in homes where the parents are so overprotective or authoritarian that they don't promote self-growth and independence in their children. These children form marriages that appear to be idyllic, because the partners seem to possess an exquisite kind of intimacy and can't bear to function without each other. In fact these relationships are often symbiotic, because the need for security is more overwhelming than any other need. They often break down when one partner outgrows his or her severe dependency needs.

It may sound paradoxical, but people who continually resist marriage because bonding with another person seems threatening and invasive may suffer from the same kind of stunted ego growth. They fear close attachments because the mere prospect of marriage triggers infantile fears of helplessness. Yet they can't bear to be alone, because their egos are so shaky. They go through life forming attachments that are destined to fail. Either they withdraw when a marriage-minded partner appears on the scene or they become attached to lovers who aren't really available. Because these failed relationships tend to work against the development of self-esteem, which is the only real way to form a healthy marriage, it may take many years to reverse these self-destructive patterns.

Always Looking, Never Finding

"I was engaged when I was twenty-one and broke it off. I had the feeling my skin would loosen and I'd flow into the other person and dissolve," says Jeanette Lindley, a slim brunette who was raised by Irish Catholic parents and married at forty-five.

Jeanette settled in Philadelphia after graduating from college and worked in an advertising agency. She was peppy and easily attracted men. But they were never marriage material. "I wanted a relationship badly, but I was too insecure to sustain one—I thought I'd lose myself—so I picked men who weren't available," she recalls. "I knew they would never cross the line and therefore I'd never have to reject them. If they were available, they were too scary, and I set limits on the time we spent together. I was afraid to have them in my life every day. But I was always upset, and it caused tremendous conflict in every area of my life."

She turned to girlfriends as sounding boards and she spent hours agonizing about men. "I put my friends through a Waring blender—and they pulled back," she recalls. "I spent so much time wondering and carrying on about men that it also took away time and energy from my job."

At thirty she started therapy and stayed with it for three years. After a two-year respite when her problems with men didn't change, she began therapy again, with a new analyst. At forty she thought she'd resolved her conflicts and moved to Houston, wanting to start over again in a new place. Shortly after she arrived, she met a forty-five-year-old pilot named Bob, a man who was separated and the father of two children. She fell madly in love with him and hung in for five years, hoping he'd get a divorce. He wouldn't, but he kept her on a string with promises he didn't intend to keep.

"He couldn't go forward—and I couldn't give him up," she explains. "It was like cutting off one of my arms. There's something fatally attractive about a person who's bad for us, and the conflict kept it going. The real truth of it is that I didn't even like him. It was like dating someone who was always leaving on a train, and hearing whistles and bells. It was like cocaine."

During this time she began an intensive search for a man she could marry, deluding herself that when she met someone suitable, she would break off with Bob. "I answered ads," she says. "I became obsessed. I went to mixers; I asked friends to fix me up; and I became so aggressive that I wasn't even that attractive. It was like a second job, and the more I did it, the less fulfilling and fun it was. The fact is I was still in love with Bob and not really available. I kept hanging on to him as my ace in the hole."

Bob finally moved to Phoenix. When he settled there, he proposed and asked her to join him. She made plans to quit her job and move. When she did, he withdrew his offer. That blow sent her to another therapist, and she finally ended the relationship. Four months later a girlfriend offered to introduce her to a man she'd met through a Personals ad because he wasn't right for her. John was fifty-seven and had been divorced for seventeen years. He was a professor of dentistry, tall and slim with a low-key manner. He was also an Irish Catholic.

John made a date with her, then broke it because he had to have a minor operation. Jeanette sent him a get-well card, but he never responded. Three months later she had a Christmas party and decided to invite him. "I got to the point where I couldn't run after men anymore," she says, "so I decided to have a party—just for my friends. I invited John simply because I needed another man."

When John entered the room, he took one look at Jeanette and headed straight for her. Within a week they were seeing each other every few days. After two weeks John said he was moving to Boston and asked her to go with him. "I asked under what circumstances," she recalls, "and he said we would get married. I said I needed at least two months to make a decision. At the end of that time I accepted. I still don't know why, but it was easy and not a problem. More than anything it was perfect timing, because I was finally ready to put aside my fears and be pursued—and once we met, he did all the chasing.

"We talked a lot about our childhood and our families. From the beginning he seemed more like a husband than a boyfriend. He was respectful and made me feel better about myself. I never worried that he wouldn't call."

I met Jeanette a week before her wedding, and she seemed calm and collected. As one of her friends put it, she had finally relaxed. "The nicest thing about our relationship now is coming together—and coming apart—and feeling it's still okay," she told me. "I used to have everything in four or five boxes and I had to open one at a time. Now I can have the whole desk drawer falling open. If I hadn't met John, I probably would have met someone else—somehow I crossed the bridge. I knew I was in good shape."

◆

Therapists say that if you tend to get caught up in self-destructive patterns, you have to break them—even if you don't understand the underlying causes. "You have to see that it's a pattern and consciously work to change your conditioning," advises Dr. Elizabeth MacAvoy, who counsels women who are in relationships with abusive men "It's very hard, because the compulsion to hang on is so strong. But the longer you stay in these relationships, the harder it is to leave because your self-esteem goes lower. And the less self-esteem you have, the harder it is to break away—it's more painful than anything else. You have to develop a program to stay away from all situations that aren't good for you—that includes girlfriends as well as boyfriends who are rejecting and abusive."

Women Who Love Too Much

Several years ago many of us read about the tragic case involving Hedda Nussbaum, a former editor, and her live-in lover, Joel Steinberg, a sadistic attorney who beat her badly and caused the death of their adopted daughter through flagrant abuse and brutality. Hedda agreed to testify against Joel and was granted immunity from prosecution. Eventually some outspoken feminists began citing Hedda's pathology as a factor contributing to the problem: After all, Hedda early on saw signs that Joel was abusive and dangerous. Instead of walking out, she began taking drugs with him and became hooked on his abuse. She invested him with magical powers and eventually lost all self-esteem. She got to the point where she couldn't distinguish right from wrong.

Many of us couldn't understand why a professional woman would put herself in such a compromising position. Yet many of us have had relationships with men who are emotionally abusive and rejecting. Some turn out to be downright pathological. Many therapists point out that women who repeatedly attach themselves to men who are either sadistic or out-of-reach have grown up in homes where a primary parent—usually a mother—is overly critical and insensitive to a child's needs.

"Women who get wounded early in childhood have a profound role model of a parent who isn't really available," explains Dr. MacAvoy. "When they meet a man who resembles the parent who was rejecting and critical, it opens up a tremendous compulsive need to get the kind of love and approval they didn't get from their parent. They follow rejecting men and it gives them the same kind of high that drug addicts get when they take cocaine."

Women who are trapped in these patterns even use pathological terms to describe their relationships with men—they see themselves as "crazy," "sick," "neurotic," and they also define their attraction as compulsive, similar to an addiction in its intense and overwhelming power.

Hooked on Bad Men

"I used to equate being in love with feeling sick to my stomach," recalls Marilyn Nelson, an outgoing public relations executive with blond hair and blue eyes who married at forty. "I would agonize all the time and put myself through a lot of anguish and physical pain.

I was always going after guys I couldn't have. I dismissed men who wanted me, and those are the ones I should have gotten involved with."

Marilyn grew up in a small town in Illinois and had what she calls a "push-pull relationship" with her mother. "She put a tremendous emphasis on appearance," recalls Marilyn. "I was a tall kid and had buck teeth and fat thighs. Then I got braces and glasses and short frizzy haircuts and I thought I was a dork. The other kids thought I was snobby because I ignored them, but the truth is I was too shy to be assertive. I was a walking bag of nerves, and my mother always criticized me and made me feel insecure—she could cut me off at the knees like no one else could."

After college Marilyn settled in Atlanta and threw herself into her work. It was a way of fueling her need for adventure and bolstering her self-esteem, and she worked her way up to a key executive position. "I was really into my job and traveled a lot, which intimidated a lot of men," she recalls. "It seemed glamorous on the surface, but the reality is I was always staying in crummy hotel rooms by myself. I remember being in Brazil once and applying makeup to a guy's face for a television promotion. I thought, I could be in Iowa or anyplace else—I never even saw Brazil."

In her thirties she dated a lot of men, but most of them were unavailable and kept her on a string. Her most important beau, Tom, was charismatic but blatantly unfaithful. Even so, she dated him for four years. "I wracked myself over him," she recalls. "We kept breaking up, but when he came back, I always went back."

When she was thirty-eight, she went to a convention where she gave a major talk to a large audience. It was her moment to shine. "I had fifteen minutes of fame, and it was great," she says. "But afterward I went back to my room and was totally alone, and I realized I had to change. I didn't want to spend the rest of my days living in empty hotel rooms."

When she returned to Atlanta, she went to a therapist. She went on a diet and lost fifteen pounds. She called up every friend she knew, asking them to introduce her to new men. "I'm sure part of it was maturing and feeling more confident because of my career," she says. "The fact that I would even go to a therapist and admit that I needed help and would pay for it was a big step. I was like an alcoholic over bad men. First I stopped seeing Tom. Then I started seeing him again and lied to my therapist because I was embarrassed to tell her. Then I went to a resort in Mexico, and it was so beautiful there that I thought, Why am I in such agony when the world is filled with natural splendor? When I returned, I broke off with him."

Several months later she began dating another man, and when she realized he was a carbon copy of Tom and her other boyfriends—he only wanted to see her at his convenience—she nipped it in the bud. "I couldn't do it anymore and decided I had to end it," she says. "I felt so strong when I did that, and when I went back to my therapist, I said, 'I can stop now. I can use the tools you gave me.'"

A year later she was on a plane and met a man she'd dated a few years ago. Joe was thirty-six, divorced, and an art director. He had previously been interested in her, but Marilyn had been so cool that he had stopped calling after five dates. "At the time it wasn't right," she recalls. "I had a wall around me because I was involved with Tom. Even though he wasn't available, I couldn't focus on anyone else."

Two months after the plane ride Joe called for a

date. "I knew this time it was right," she recalls. "I had changed my attitude and I was open to a really nice guy." Then she had to cancel their second date because she was sick. Joe offered to make dinner for her. "He could have gone out with another woman that night, but he cared about me. And I knew from the way he felt about his mother that he would want to be married and settled. Joe's mother was his best friend—she taught him to cook and be self-sufficient."

They dated steadily after that night and bought a townhouse together within three months. Six months later they married. "Joe was always attentive and always available," she says in retrospect. "He was the first man I felt really comfortable with. I know he will do anything for me and I can count on him when the chips are down."

◆

Women who start out in their twenties with insecure egos may experience years of unhappy encounters with men who wear down their self-confidence instead of shoring it up. The real problem, according to psychologist Stanton Peele, stems from a lack of secure underpinnings in life, and therefore the solution is complex and takes time. It often involves developing inner resources and a sense of competency in areas that may have little to do with romantic relationships. "To build our sense of strength and purpose we have to apply ourselves in a concerted way to pursuits which may not always be completely pleasant, but which offer us something of substance when we master them," he advises. "Only through working hard at learning to do something well, something which is important to us and to other people, can we generate the competence and self-possession that will make a difference in our lives."[10]

"This Can't Be Love Because I Feel So Well"

Not all women who have unhappy encounters with men are rent with neurotic conflicts. It's only when all your experiences are painful and have a repetitive nature that internal conflicts may exist. After all it's virtually impossible to escape some upsetting romantic experiences if you are actively dating and willing to explore relationships with men.

Many times it's difficult to let these unsatisfactory relationships go—or evaluate them properly—because a host of social and cultural forces work against us. The male shortage feeds into these scenarios; it is hard to meet men and form any connection at all, and there's a tendency to rationalize these no-win relationships because the specter of loneliness seems more awesome than the anguish of hanging in.

But there are other cultural factors that encourage us to weather stormy relationships. Many classical dramas and novels abound with stories in which passion is characterized as an emotional state involving distress and euphoria. Romeo and Juliet, Antony and Cleopatra, and Cathy and Heathcliff in *Wuthering Heights* are some of the heroes and heroines who experienced alternating cycles of agony and ecstasy, torment and elation, because their passion was never consummated.

Even though rigid class structures, warring families, grievous misunderstandings, and a simple lack of communication were the various reasons for these unfulfilled unions, the impact on us is still the same: Love is filled with wild emotional swings. "I want you, but I can't have you" and "I can't live with you, but I can't live without you" are commonplace themes in many popular songs.

No wonder we tend to confuse high anxiety and love. When we experience trepidation, despair, and angst, we often think we're experiencing the inevitable pangs of love. Love, we're told, is supposed to hurt. Pain is cleansing and even purifying. If love doesn't make us suffer, how real can it be?

Most modern therapists, however, stress that healthy love can develop only when people have a high regard for themselves and realistic expectations. Maybe that's why all the women I interviewed said that when they achieved a certain level of self-confidence and were happy with themselves, they became receptive to men who valued them. They were also able to value these men. We've heard it so many times, but you do have to love yourself before you can allow someone else to love you—and before you can love someone worth loving.

"I Wasn't Going to Let Myself Down"

When Diane Lindsay went off to a bridge tournament in Kansas City, she'd decided that marriage wasn't in her future. She was forty-seven at the time. "I'd gotten to the point of saying there were not too many men out there for me and I decided not to run to singles events anymore because I didn't like the men I met," says Diane, a high-powered executive with an assertive manner. "I didn't want to become like the women who are jaded by three or four bad love affairs. I decided

I was comfortable being single and in control of my life. Someone else can't make you happy—you have to be happy with yourself—and I wasn't going to let myself down."

Diane grew up in a small town in California and went to an elite women's college where she was active in school government. She was also quite attractive. "I was very popular," she says. "But I dated more like a little girl than a woman. I'd find men who would put up with me no matter what I did."

After graduating she got an MBA from Harvard and settled in Los Angeles, where her two married sisters and widowed mother lived. She also began working for a major corporation in data processing.

Diane is not the sit-at-home type. She developed a wide network of male and female friends and was out almost every night, to the ballet, concerts, plays, lectures or films. She also became a competitive bridge and golf player.

In her twenties she met a man who wanted to marry her, but she wasn't ready—she was too involved with her own activities. In her thirties she was engaged for six weeks; then her fiancé pulled out. Nonetheless Diane continued to date a lot and had short-term relationships with men, which collapsed for various reasons. When she was forty-two, she met a thirty-six-year-old psychologist. "I thought I was in love," she says. "He was perfect, on paper. He was divorced and had a son. I really worked at the relationship, but he was so angry underneath that he mistreated me and said cruel things. In retrospect I see that I fell in love with his image and not the person. Even so, it was very painful to let go. I was disappointed because I had thought I was a good judge of people. After we broke up, I just decided to live my life the best I could and thought marriage wasn't in the stars."

At the bridge tournament in Kansas City she was matched up with a married man from Des Moines. Peter was eight years younger than Diane, tall, and even-tempered. They played well together and Diane was drawn to him. She figured he would be a friend.

Several weeks later he invited her to be his doubles partner in a match in Dallas. They spent an evening together dancing. They played bridge and golf the next day. Then Diane invited him to play bridge with her in a tournament in Bermuda. He rejected her invitation and said that if he went to Bermuda, he would take his wife along. "That was like a slap in the face," she recalls. "It really upset me, and I wound up overeating that night. I didn't expect to see him again—nor did I want to. A week later he sent me a long letter saying that he had planned to have an affair with me in Dallas but that he had gotten cold feet. He also said he was jealous of my life and my self-sufficiency. His wife was a sweet woman who doted on him."

Then he sent her another letter saying he really cared about her, not because of the sexual attraction but because he thought they could really communicate. Shortly after that, Peter visited Diane in Los Angeles while his wife was away. "I sat down on my bed," she recalls, "and said, 'Do I want a weekend fling with a married man?' I decided it might be fun and I decided I could handle it."

During the weekend he said his marriage wasn't in great shape and that he either had to work it out or end it. "I encouraged him to work it out," says Diane. "I made no demands on him after he left."

Several weeks later he called and said he'd separated from his wife. Then he came back to Los Angeles, but when he talked about getting a divorce, Diane got nervous. "I didn't want him to feel that he was getting a divorce with the idea that I would be his woman," says Diane. "But he seemed determined and was divorced within two months. We began commuting on weekends, and I went along without thinking in permanent terms. I figured he would want to sow his wild oats, but he said he'd been alone the past five years of his life and didn't want space. 'Alone,' I said, 'is not the same as free.'"

In December he had unexpected brain surgery, and that brought them closer together. After his operation he proposed. "I said I had to think," says Diane. "Did I really want to change my life in a dramatic way? Would I try to take charge, because I'm very strong? For all our mutual interests we were very different."

She finally said yes, and the day after she accepted, her mother died suddenly. Peter came to Los Angeles immediately and was at her side throughout the crisis. They married several months later.

"He's not like most of the men I was used to dating," says Diane. "He's from the Midwest and not sophisticated. But it was wonderful to meet a man who really pursued me. There was a lot of caring and attention on his part. His family says he has changed in a positive way—he's become more outgoing and communicative.

"We're a good balance," she says. "I'm the champagne. He's the beer. He was very supportive when my mother died. There was never great upheaval—from the minute we began dating, he was always there for me."

◆

One reason why women often meet the men they marry when they least expect to is that they are no longer needy, defensive, or compulsively looking for a man who will fill a void in their life. "This lack of desperation communicates itself subtly but surely to others as an attractive and desirable quality," says Stanton Peele, "for people generally find it reassuring to relate to those who are already certain of their own value."[11]

We may not be able to control our environment, but we can control ourselves. We have the choice to feel good about ourselves. We have the choice to be happy. And we have the choice to reject men who are abusive, remote, and out of bounds.

SIX

Shopping for a Spouse

Getting your act together and developing self-esteem are critical if you want a healthy relationship with a man. But readiness isn't always enough. You can't depend on blind dates, parties, or chance encounters to meet the man of your dreams. At least that's what Elena Kovac decided just before she turned thirty-nine.

"The bells went off," recalls Elena, an animated blonde who was working as a financial analyst at the time. "Suddenly I had the kind of feeling you have when you're in the hospital and no one's there—and it wasn't going to get better, it was only going to get worse. I decided to look for a man who would be with me in the long run. I took the point of view that there were at least a hundred men who could be suitable.

He didn't have to be the love of my life or even my intellectual equal. He just had to do three things: He had to marry me; he had to stay with me; and he had to hug me. I gave myself a year to find a husband, and by the time I reached forty, I was married."

Elena was born in Poland and emigrated to New York City with her parents when she was five. They spoke Polish at home, so she became fluent in her mother tongue. Throughout the years she maintained ties with her relatives in Eastern Europe.

When she turned eighteen she married an immigrant from Cyprus. The marriage lasted two years. When it was over, she went back to school and got a degree in business so that she could get a high-paying job in the corporate world.

In her twenties Elena dated a lot, but without any intention of marrying. She was wary of making another mistake and didn't want to be tied down. Instead she threw herself into her career, traveled a lot, went to the ballet and concerts, and became active in feminist groups.

"I always thought I had time and would meet the great passion of my life tomorrow," she recalls. "I wanted a man who was cosmopolitan, elegantly dressed, well educated, successful in his work, and a world traveler. I wanted the whole American dream. And I thought I would fall into it naturally. The problem is, I kept falling into the wrong thing with the wrong person. He was either married, or he couldn't make a commitment, or he wanted to spend all his money on a boat. I used to wake up in bed with men I loved—but didn't like."

So Elena kept on dating and having casual affairs. When the outbreak of AIDS occurred, she cut out one-night stands and became more cautious about screening dates, since some of her previous boy-friends had been active in the arts and were bisexual.

She also revised what she wanted in a spouse and began looking upon marriage as a practical transaction instead of a passionate love affair. She would have gone to a matchmaker, but she couldn't find one. So she decided to make her own match.

She began by getting herself fired from her job. It had involved four hours of commuting each day and didn't leave her with enough energy to maintain an active social life. She took on free-lance work to keep herself afloat.

Then she placed a Personals ad in a Polish news-paper in New York City, because she thought new immigrants would be more marriage-minded and stable than many of the men she'd been dating. She also figured that she and they would have a heritage in common. She received thirty responses and met all the men. She started dating one of them—a separated man, who had left a wife and two children in Poland. When he refused to get a divorce, she dropped him. Soon after, a woman friend from Poland encouraged her to put an ad in a newspaper in Warsaw. The ad she devised was simple enough. She gave her height in centimeters and her weight and described herself as an attractive, American college-educated blonde, who was looking for a nondrinking, nonsmoking eligible man. She also requested a photo. She dictated the ad over the phone to the husband of her friend. He agreed to place it, collect the responses, and send them to her.

She received one hundred and fifty letters and screened them with input from friends and family. She finally selected ten. "Some, I liked the pictures," she says. "Some, I liked the letters. And some of the men had practical trades that would lend themselves to being in America."

Then she bought a cheap ticket on a charter plane to Warsaw during Thanksgiving week. She sent postcards to the men she'd selected, asking each one to meet her at her hotel. She allotted two hours for each man and set up three appointments a day.

Her plane was delayed in Belgrade due to heavy fog, so she missed her first day of appointments. Three men didn't show up. She wound up meeting an engineer, who liked telling dirty jokes, and a pilot, who drank too much. She dismissed both of them. The third man turned out to be a thirty-nine-year-old sailor named Stephen who had never been married. "Stephen was standing there in a blue uniform looking very young and very lost," she recalls with a romantic gleam in her eye. "He had made a deal with one of his friends to take a month off so that he could come and meet me. He worked as an electrician on a ship—the same ship my father had worked on in the merchant marines—so we had a lot in common.

"He showed me pictures of his travels, and he booked a room in the same hotel so that we could have dinner the next night. He didn't make sexual advances—he gave me time. I enjoyed him a lot, and after I left Poland, we wrote letters. His were very warm and filled with poetry."

The following January Elena went back to Poland to visit Stephen, and he proposed. "He was very romantic," she recalls. "We spent a few days together and there was a physical attraction. He's a warm, attractive, friendly person, who likes to have fun, and he has traveled the world. He's a good companion; he wanted a family; he'd been around; he was Catholic and didn't believe in divorce."

They married the following spring in an old-fashioned church wedding, because Stephen insisted. Elena got a job at a major insurance company, and they rented an apartment in an area of Brooklyn where there was a community of Polish people. Stephen got jobs as an electrician almost immediately, earning ten dollars an hour.

"I used to think I would be more compatible with another executive," she says, "but Stephen was raised on a farm, and he doesn't have hang-ups about my working, because he grew up in an environment where everyone worked. He doesn't see me as competitive and has no problem cooking or helping around the house. Blue-collar people are simpler and easier to forge a marriage with. There's an understanding that survival is at stake, death is around the corner, and old age involves sickness and difficulty. They have a closer relationship to nature and the harsh winters of life. And I can't get the same kind of closeness and hugging and kissing from men who are caught up in their careers. If for any reason this marriage doesn't work out, I'll go back to Poland or another European country and do exactly the same thing again. Or I'll do it here. I could have found someone here if I'd been willing to spend more time looking."

Personals Ads: Custom-made Romance

Elena's pragmatic attitude toward marriage may be upsetting to women who feel that it is humiliating, coldhearted, or just plain unromantic to shop for a husband. Yet most of us know that if we want to find a job, we have to market ourselves aggressively and plot careful strategies to get interviews with potential employers. In the world of romance, however, our old-fashioned values and behavior often prevail. We either want to meet men in natural ways—or we want men to seek us out. Diligently planning ways to meet men is considered by many to be distasteful, brazen, unfeminine—and smacking of desperation.

Or is it?

When Mrs. Bennet, the well-meaning mother in Jane Austen's novel *Pride and Prejudice*, discovered that Mr. Bingley, a young man of fortune and stature, had just moved into the community, she nagged her husband to invite him to dinner right away so that one of her five daughters could entice him before all her neighbors' daughters had a chance to compete. Mrs. Bennet was hardly the first mother to take an active posture in recruiting eligible suitors for her daughters. For centuries and centuries women, often abetted by their parents, have devised artful methods to meet, seduce, and conquer desirable bachelors.

The main difference between the techniques our mothers and grandmothers used—and the various methods women are employing today—is that strategies such as Personals ads are anonymous, commercial—and riskier—than the genteel practices of inviting men to private dinners, teas, and balls.

In many traditional areas of America, ads still summon up the stigmas that developed when Lonely Hearts columns were viewed as last resorts for unhappy men and women who couldn't fend for themselves. When I decided to place an ad in *New York* magazine, a popular upscale city journal, my mother was horrified: "Oh Barbara," she said, "you don't need to do that—do you?" She was also frightened: Was it really safe to make a date with a virtual stranger who could turn out to be a rapist, murderer, liar, or lunatic?

My mother grew up in an era when women from good families didn't place ads in weeklies to find dates. She met all her beaux at college or through friends. The idea of meeting a man who wasn't screened by a third party was terrifying to her and her peers.

Times have changed. Even though most women say they prefer meeting men through personal introductions, private parties, or work-related events, it's difficult to rely on these means if you live in a crowded metropolis, where thousands of single people pass each other like ships in the night—or even if you live in a small city, where it's hard to meet men who aren't part of your social set. It's particularly tough if you're a working woman and don't have the time or energy to run to singles parties and cocktail lounges or to entertain.

Men have similar problems. Many work long hours and don't like party hopping or hanging around bars. Many shy away from dating women who work in their offices because it sets up complications. Even men who are flooded with names of eligible women to call for dates say they prefer the anonymity of meeting women without the intervention of a friend—or client—who will monitor the interaction.

As a result the system of social networking through the Personals has become a staple of social life in many cities, particularly large metropolitan areas, such as New York City, Boston, Philadelphia, Washington, D.C., and Los Angeles. In these urban areas the density of single people, the stresses of high-pressured jobs, and the difficulties of commuting have made ads appealing and efficient as a way of meeting.

"I really wanted to meet a woman and get into a relationship when I came to New York," said a forty-five-year-old executive who placed and answered ads to find dates. "Ideally I'd like to meet a woman naturally, but you don't have that flexibility in New York, and ads give me a greater spectrum of women to meet. And I don't mind killing two hours over a drink. In the course of two years I've met thirty women through the ads—and I dated two for a long period of time."

The men and women who use ads most frequently are in their thirties and forties. They tend to be more cut off from ready-made social networks than people in their twenties, who still have lots of single friends, and opt for parties and even bars as a way of meeting others.

"A lot of our advertisers are divorced men and women over thirty-five who want to do it right the second time around," says Dayna Zimmerman, the classified-advertising manager of *Boston Magazine*, a popular urban weekly that now carries about two hundred ads a month, two-thirds of them placed by women and one-third by men. "It's become an acceptable way of networking here, but many people are still uncomfortable about admitting that they have met someone that way," she explains. "They're usually professional people with college degrees, and they seem to be looking for a woman or man with similar interests. A lot of them use the word *counterpart* to describe what they're looking for. Cute, catchy ads have the best response rate. People who seem to be open and don't limit themselves, or who don't put in laundry lists, have the best chance of meeting someone."

According to advertising managers, Personals ads are still taking root in medium-sized cities in the South and Midwest, partly because the old-fashioned stigmas and norms prevail in these areas. Personals have become popular in remote areas, however, where it's unusually difficult to find partners. Two years ago

The New York Times published a feature article on networking through Personals ads in the farmlands, where men typically outnumber women. "The ladies go off to the cities to find jobs and the fellows stay home to run the farms—it's hard for a person on the farm to find the time to go around looking for a date," said William E. Blauvelt, publisher of *Country Connections*, a newsletter based in Superior, Nebraska, with about two thousand subscribers, two-thirds of them men.[1] *Singles in Agriculture* and *Rural Networking for Remote Singles* are two other publications that have developed to service the romantic needs of farmers who are isolated from social contacts. As a result men place many more ads in these papers than women because they have few ways to meet dates.

But in the large cities where Personals have caught on, ads placed by women tend to outnumber ads placed by men. The reasons are fairly clear-cut: Most women have a tougher time finding partners than men because they are hesitant to collect the names of eligible men from friends and ask them out. And many women are inhibited about calling men for dates after they meet them at parties.

When women do answer ads that are placed by men, they often don't get many responses to their letters, primarily because the men are usually inundated with replies and can answer only a handful.

Women in their late thirties and forties, for example, who place ads in *New York*, which has a readership of about 1.5 million, typically receive twenty to forty responses. Men who place ads say they receive at least eighty responses, and some receive as many as one hundred and fifty. The same pattern persists in Washington, D.C., Los Angeles, and other cities with many single people. In smaller cities men as well as women receive fewer responses, because the local magazines have fewer readers. But men still receive more responses than women who are their peers.

A friend of mine in Rochester, New York, told me she placed an ad in a local newspaper, describing herself as a divorced mother and medical researcher in her forties. She received eight responses. One of her former boyfriends, a divorced man in his early sixties, placed an ad that ran below hers in the same issue. He received fifteen responses. Even so, she was happy with the process. She met several men she wouldn't have met on her own, since they lived in different suburbs and didn't frequent the parties she goes to.

Women who succeed in getting responses when they answer ads say that they write careful notes that respond exactly to what a man is seeking. Many enclose attractive but not overly seductive photos. A lot of men do request pictures and, because they receive so many responses from women, they won't answer letters that aren't accompanied by photographs.

Men who answer ads don't usually write elaborate letters, but if they have a stable profession and are in the appropriate age group, women will often call them. As a result many men who have used the ads as a way of dating prefer to answer ads instead of placing them because it's easy, effective—and free. "Why do I answer ads? That's simple—it's cheaper," explained a forty-five-year-old editor. "Placing ads can get expensive after a while, and I tend to get responses from most of the women I write to. I rule out ads that require a photo because that seems like a meat market to me, and I tend to answer those that are well written, short, and sound as though we will have common interests."

Other men say they prefer answering ads because it gives them a feeling of control. "When I placed an ad, I got over eighty responses and it was too confusing to sort them all out," said a forty-four-year-old accountant. "When I answer ads, I can control the flow, and I can decide whom to respond to. I tend to look for women near my age who are very bright and creative. I usually get a seventy- to eighty-percent response. I call about a third of them and tend to meet half the women I talk to on the phone. The last time I did this, I met about twenty women, and three I liked—three liked me. Then I met Susan, and by the time we sat down at the table, I knew we were attracted to each other, and we dated for a long time."

Many men say they answer ads that are short, descriptive, snappy, and direct. They avoid ads that are verbose, indirect, or gimmicky. If they are really marriage-minded or looking for a relationship, they veer away from ads that are overtly sexual or seductive.

Many men are also selective and respond to only one or two ads from an issue. A year ago a friend and I accidentally placed an ad in the same issue of *New York*. We are the same age and we both have Ph.D.'s. She used as a lead, "Green-eyed Russian professor," and explained in the text that she was elegant, divorced, and interested in the arts and gourmet cooking. I used "Attractive blond journalist" as a lead and went on to say I liked tennis, the arts, and traveling.

We each asked for men who were well educated and in their forties or fifties. (We didn't state our age.) We each received about twenty-five letters, but we received only two letters from the same men. We each called five men.

She began dating a divorced man in his fifties, an advertising executive, and they went out for about five months. It was the first relationship she'd had in four years.

I decided not to meet the first three men I called.

I met the fourth because we had a long conversation on the phone and I liked his energy. He turned out to be a tall, handsome, divorced executive in his early fifties. We dated steadily for three months, then he panicked and bolted. He wanted a close relationship —until he discovered that he was in one.

My friend and I broke up with our respective beaux about the same time. We decided to place another ad and wound up in the same issue again. We again received about twenty-five responses each. A few were the same men who had responded to our previous ads; a few men answered both of our ads. But most of the responses we received were new and did not overlap.

She met four men—a businessman who took her to a classy restaurant on their first meeting, an investment banker whom she saw a few times, and two others she didn't like. I met a physician, clearly distinguished but too old; a handsome real estate executive with a degree from Yale, who was not for me; a film producer whom I dated twice; and a divorced engineer in his early fifties—the kind of sane, solid, sensible man I used to dismiss as boring. He wooed me ardently for several weeks—and then he disappeared.

Ads can be an easy and relatively inexpensive way of refueling your social life without the hassle of going to bars or mixers. But they're not a panacea. Men often lie about their age and their appearance. If they're in their fifties or sixties, they often knock off five years. They usually describe themselves as good-looking even when they're fat and paunchy. Many are simply window-shopping while they are trying to resolve another relationship. Many sound intriguing on the phone but turn out to be disappointing in person.

A year ago I answered an ad by a man who described himself as a successful businessman with a love of the arts. He wanted to meet a woman in her late thirties, and even though I said I was in my forties, he decided to call me.

When I met him, I found out why. He was well over sixty, and his hands shook slightly when he picked up a glass of apple juice—he didn't drink liquor. He was genuinely well educated and accomplished, but not at all in my sphere. More to the point he really wasn't interested in meeting anyone. He'd placed the same ad in two consecutive issues and had received 367 responses, ranging from chic models and actresses to lawyers. He called fifty women, met twelve, and didn't find anyone he wanted to see more than once. Our entire meeting lasted forty-five minutes—and I breathed a sigh of relief when it was over.

A lot of men use the Personals simply to keep busy. Others are so flooded with responses that they never focus on any woman at all. There are also men who use ads for devious scams: They may be married men trying to get an affair going on the side, or they may be sexual miscreants.

Recently several articles have appeared narrating the scary tales of women who have been brutalized or raped by men they met through ads.[2] These incidents are extremely rare—and they can occur with any man you date who hasn't been screened by a reliable third party.

But since the men you meet through ads are complete unknowns, caution is advised: Don't give out your last name when you write letters to ads placed by men or even in an initial talk on the phone. When you meet, try to get a business card and set up a date in a public place not near your home.

It's also advisable to ask some pertinent questions

to verify a man's credibility: What company does he work for? (You can easily check that out.) What is his home phone? (Married men won't give it out.) What clubs or organizations does he belong to? Where did he go to college? Be sure to see a man at least twice before you invite him into your living room. At all costs avoid going to his apartment. And don't go away on a weekend until you have spent a block of time with him.

I've never had a frightening experience with a man I met through an ad. Neither have my friends. I've had more unpleasant episodes with men I met at private parties or on blind dates. In my view the main downside of dating through the ads is that most of the men you meet are not suitable for you and you waste a couple of hours with them. Love may be blind, but chemistry is not.

Men also get their share of rude shocks or dour experiences when they ask out women who sound appealing on the phone. Often they are stuck with a bill they don't want to pay. Women also lie about their age and their appearance. Men say that "shapely" is a euphemism for fat. Some women are also window-shopping or are not really focused on developing a relationship.

One friend of mine said he answered about six ads, each in a different issue of a magazine. He's very good-looking and enclosed a photo, so all the women called him. One woman he met—a sleek blonde from Denmark—invited him to participate in a ménage à trois and asked him to bring the third. (He was tempted, but the fear of AIDS restrained him.) Another woman was an artist who lived in Greenwich Village. She stripped on their first date and asked him to paint mosaics on her back. (His aesthetic impulses overcame his fear of disease in that case.) A third pestered him with phone calls for weeks after they met —even though he made it clear he wasn't interested.

Anyone who has dated through the ads has a story to tell: Just about everyone receives some letters from men or women in prison, or people who are in stale marriages and looking for affairs, or people who are just plain losers or as bland as Wonder Bread.

The men and women who tend to be the most successful in finding mates through ads are people who know what they want—and who keep going until they find it.

"I Got Exactly What I Wanted"

When Sandra Campel placed her fourth ad in a popular magazine, she was forty-five and knew exactly what she wanted in a man. Sandra, a soft-spoken textbook editor, is sweet, generous, and even-tempered. She settled in Boston after graduating from Mount Holyoke. She dated frequently through the years and had several long-term relationships, however none of her boyfriends would make commitments, and she was too insecure to end the affairs or make demands.

"I did a lot of the giving and didn't get as much in return," she recalls. "I always thought I should try harder—instead of thinking what the men could be doing. I didn't have a good enough opinion of my own value and would think, If I'm really patient, the guy will change his mind, and it will turn out okay. I also hung in because I knew there would be a long dry spell if we separated. I figured I wouldn't find the perfect person and used that as a justification for staying in relationships that weren't working out."

When Sandra turned forty, she had a rude jolt. She

discovered she had breast cancer and had a modified radical mastectomy. The trauma fueled her own sense of inadequacy and made her even more willing to put up with men who didn't fulfill her needs. "Women our age don't have an easy time finding men," she says. "When this happened, I thought, What man would deal with this on top of all the other things? So it was really tough. I also wanted a baby and decided that if I didn't marry, I would adopt a child on my own. So I began working overtime to earn more money."

Three years later she had a recurrence of cancer that was even more upsetting and painful. She received massive doses of chemotherapy and began seeing a therapist who specialized in helping cancer patients. "My hair fell out, I had some bouts of nausea, and I went on medical disability," she says. "I began thinking that there were things I was doing to myself emotionally to bring it on. I had been working overtime and free-lancing to generate more income so that I could adopt a child, and it created a lot of stress. I decided to stop working so hard and gave up the idea of adopting a child. A lot became unraveled."

As she began to feel stronger about herself, she placed a Personals ad in a popular magazine describing herself as a "Cancer Patient Without Partner" who was upbeat, warm, and a professional. She received fifteen responses and met four men: One was a radiologist; another tried to proposition her at lunch; the other two were simply not for her.

Six months later she placed another ad, but this time she changed the lead to "Mt. Holyoke Grad" and omitted all mention of her illness. She received about forty responses. The next fall she placed a similar ad that also drew about forty responses. "I kept doing it because I was getting better at it, and I figured the more ads I placed, the more men I would meet and the more possibilities I would have to meet someone right. After all, I've shopped for everything else I wanted until I found what I was looking for. Why should the most important relationship in my life be any different?"

Her therapist helped her rebuild her self-confidence and work through a lot of her internal conflicts that came to the fore when she was stricken with cancer. "I began having a better opinion of myself," she says. "I began demanding more of everyone—employers as well as doctors—and decided to open myself up to the possibility that I could find the kind of mate I really wanted. My life was too short to waste on men who weren't suitable."

Shortly after she turned forty-five, she designed a new ad:

Slim, Leggy, Blue-Eyed—Warm, well-educated, articulate woman editor, 40's, with high-tech spirit, creative mind, traditional values, and romantic heart. Wishes to be wooed by tall, slim, intelligent, outgoing, sensitive, emotionally mature man with sense of humor, 35 plus, to build close friendship and lasting love relationship.

"Each time I placed an ad, I put in something that I liked about myself," she recalls. "This time I did some real thinking and decided to ask for a man who was emotionally mature and wouldn't run away. I took some risks with the lead, because I emphasized my legs, but I thought it would attract attention. I also decided to look for a younger man. I'd always dated men my own age, or older, but it dawned on me that that wasn't a good mix, since older men tended to be more traditional in their male-female roles. But I didn't stress his profession. I used to be fixated on marrying a lawyer, and it took me years to get away from that stereotype. I still wanted someone who was well educated, but he didn't have to be Ivy League, and he didn't have to be a lawyer. I wanted someone who was happy with himself, confident, and open about his feelings."

She received forty responses again and graded them in terms of their desirability. The first one she answered was a handwritten note from a forty-three-year-old divorced editor who was educated in the Midwest. He liked classical music and had a home in the country. They met for a drink at a hotel near her apartment where she typically met men from the ads.

"Within the first hour we discovered it was easy talking," she recalls. "We had a lot in common regarding children, politics, relationships, family, and work. There was a tremendous rapport. He asked me to dinner, and on the way to the restaurant I took his arm, and he thought that was terrific. I made it a policy not to bring up the health issue on a first date—I wanted a man to get to know me first. But over dinner he mentioned a cousin who had breast cancer, and he talked about her in such a sympathetic way that I thought if I didn't mention this right away, it would spoil what was building up. When I told him, he took my hand and squeezed it, and I sighed. It's out. Now I have nothing to hide."

After dinner they had coffee in her apartment, and he said he'd call. "I had a sense he would," says Sandra. "So I decided I wouldn't call the next man on my list until I saw if he did. He called two days later, and we had three more dates. Then he went off on a business trip. When he returned, I invited him over to dinner. It was a Saturday night, and it cemented everything. Mark is very affectionate, verbally expressive, and he likes to talk about his feelings. He's also happy with himself. Men who are struggling with their image can't stick it out in a relationship."

They began seeing each other several times a week. Two and a half months later he moved in. Then he took her on a trip to the Pacific Northwest and proposed. They married the following August. "The problem used to be that I was too willing to compromise," says Sandra. "I got into relationships that weren't satisfying. Before I met Mark, I developed a clear idea of what I wanted and I had the courage to ask for it. He filled the bill in every way. In retrospect I'm glad I waited because I got exactly what I wanted."

Dating Services: A Cap for Every Bottle?

Matchmaking services are even older than Lonely Hearts columns. Maybe that's why they carry more stigmas than Personals ads. Many people still view them as an outpost for lost souls who are weird, desperate, unloved, or incapable of managing their own lives.

Midge Peiser, a forty-four-year-old social worker and therapist who lives in Miami, used to feel that way. A peppy redhead with blue eyes, she always thought that dating services were too downbeat for her. She met most of her boyfriends at parties or through her work or at beach resorts. But when she saw a small ad in a newspaper for a Jewish dating service that charged only thirty-nine dollars and guaranteed her eleven names of possible suitors over a nine-month period, she decided to gamble.

"I had tried everything else—including the Personals—and had not dated a man for ten months," she explains. "I was working too hard to go to singles events, and on weekends I was exhausted. After a long lean spell I was up for doing something, and signing up with this agency seemed easy and cheap. Most dating services turned me off, since you had to subject yourself to a video and they charged too much. I didn't want to spend tons of money."

She went in for an interview and filled out a simple card that asked her to list her name, profession, age, education, and interests. She asked for a man who was Jewish, college-educated, divorced, and forty-four or younger. Within two weeks she received five names. One was a tax accountant, two years younger than Midge. He was still living in the same house as his wife and daughter, but he dated women— openly—since a legal divorce was in the works. Bernie and Midge talked on the phone about four times before they met, and both of them felt a real connection. "Bernie was coming out of a marriage and he didn't know anything about the singles network," says Midge. "He had dated four or five women and was ending a nine-month relationship. He signed up with the agency two months before I did and he had met fourteen women before we talked, but he didn't connect with any of them."

Bernie wasn't exactly Midge's fantasy mate, but Midge had given up on fantasies long ago. He was tall, had dark curly hair, and exuded a blunt kind of macho charm. The latter was partly due to his tough accent, a carryover from his upbringing in New York City, and it made Midge cringe initially.

Bernie married when he was nineteen and had one daughter. As soon as the child was born, his wife became totally focused on her. Bernie went into therapy for five years and in the process made an emotional leap that his wife couldn't match or understand. They grew farther and farther apart; there were constant fights and conflicts; they had almost no sex; and they decided to divorce.

"We were married but we never had a relationship," he explains. "For years I was only a paycheck. After we separated, I went out a lot—just for sex. After a while that got boring and I wanted to find someone to link up with. I don't like being alone. I like sharing."

So Bernie signed up with the service because he didn't know a lot of single women. "How bad could it be for forty bucks?" he says. "Then the phone started ringing off the hook. I began feeling like a commodity and could have screwed myself across the city. But I didn't want that. Midge attracted me because I could really talk to her."

They dated steadily, but Midge didn't mention marriage. A month later he told her he wasn't going to call anyone else on his list, even though she wasn't ready to make the same commitment so soon.

"He was consistent from the beginning and never left me hanging," says Midge. "I never had to wait very long for him to call. He was also warm and sensitive, a stable worker, and there was no game playing. He was bright, and I hung in. I didn't know what was going to happen but decided to give it a try. And it was smooth because he was very open and we talked about everything."

They married three years after they met. They're now living happily in Midge's one-bedroom apartment.

◆

The kind of matchmaking service that Midge and Bernie used has now been outpaced by elaborate—and expensive—referral services, which are outfitted with therapists, videotapes, counselors, and sophisticated psychological tests—all designed to give clients exactly what they want without the risks of meeting blind dates who haven't been screened by a legitimate third party. These services charge anywhere from around $250 to fees in the thousands. Some large-scale bureaus hold parties and informal gatherings for members. They operate not only as dating services, but as social clubs with a specialized referral service available to members.

People Resources, for example, is a singles club and members have access to a library consisting of written profiles and videos of all its members. It charges a sliding scale of roughly $1,650 to $3,000 to its three-thousand members, who range in age from twenty-five to fifty-five. The ratio is about 5 to 4, women to men. Clients first meet with counselors. After paying a fee they are entitled to self-select potential dates by studying a large loose-leaf binder filled with detailed biographies and photos of other members. They may also view videotapes of members.

After this screening process they can issue an invitation to a person of their choice. The person who receives the invitation can accept or decline. He or she is also welcome to view a videotape of the person extending the invitation. People Resources sponsors lectures, museum tours, theater outings, and wine-tasting events, where members can meet one another informally. "People use our service to conduct an organized search for partners and to take control of their lives," says Cynthia Gamesik, assistant to the president. "Most women are looking for special relationships, and being able to be selective about their dates gives them a real confidence about themselves. Men come in to expand their social opportunities; often they've tried other avenues that haven't worked.

The city is a hard place to meet other single people, and we make it easier."

It's difficult to assess the value of these services because the people who run them claim that many members date and marry. I've met men and women, however, who have used these services, and the reviews are mixed.

One very attractive woman lawyer, who signed up when she was thirty-four, said she met about fifteen men in the course of a year. She was delighted with the service, since she rarely met men on her own. Other women I've talked to, most of them in their forties, are less enthusiastic.

One friend, a Rubenesque redhead with an outgoing personality and a wide circle of male and female friends, paid $1,500 to a video service in Manhattan because she thought it would pep up her social life in an easy way. She received invitations from eight men that she declined; she sent eight invitations to men who didn't respond to her. She wound up meeting three men and saw one of them twice. Another woman, a striking brunette in her late forties, met three men in six months. She voiced a typical complaint: She didn't feel she got her money's worth.

One problem with video services is that they self-select men and women who look good on camera. Unfortunately, being photogenic is not everyone's strong point. Conversely, photogenic people are often drab-looking in real life. I've interviewed a lot of high-powered film stars and I can tell you that, dressed in jogging pants and a sweatshirt, Cher does not exude great sex appeal. Only the rare actor or actress is a natural beauty. Liv Ullmann and Gregory Peck don't need makeup and proper lighting to shine, yet even they know that to maximize their features for the camera, they must rely on professional makeup artists and photographers. If you decide to use any service that relies on photographs or videotapes—or if you simply want to enclose a photo when you answer a Personals ad—it's wise to spend some money on a person who can help you highlight your strengths for the camera.

"If it's important enough, go to a professional photographer who will accentuate your positives," advises Jim Blue, a divorced marketing executive who explored Personals ads and a dating service before he remarried. "Reagan doesn't wear ties that stand out, because he's a good-looking man. Other men accessorize. People are visually oriented. When you buy a product in a supermarket, you often buy the ones that stand out. Why should selecting a date be any different when you're inundated with possibilities?"

But the real problem for women is not that dating services rely on videos and visuals but that many men in their forties and fifties are still loathe to use these services.

"It would make me feel as though I couldn't meet a woman on my own, and that wouldn't give me a good feeling about myself," said a divorced man in his early fifties. "I don't even like the Personals, but at least they operate in an open market without any subterfuge. Besides, they don't cost as much."

Men in their thirties are more likely to use dating services because they are less traditional. Men who are recently divorced and are novices in the dating world may also spend money on them.

Since many dating services are underused by men in their forties and fifties, women angling for men in these age groups may not receive many invitations—or acceptances when they issue invitations. When this happens, women tend to personalize these rejections as a sign of their own inadequacy. Yet it often reflects the fact that there aren't enough men in the rosters.

Before you join a dating service, insist on finding out as much as possible about the process and membership. Ask to speak with other members. Know what you're getting into. If you do hand over a lot of money without asking appropriate questions, you might be setting yourself up for disappointment. Dating services that sponsor parties, trips, lectures, and informal gatherings are probably more valuable than those that simply act as referral services. At the very least you'll meet new women friends and have access to enjoyable activities.

Custom-made Matchmakers: Service or Sham?

Individual matchmakers with customized services have also come into vogue in large cities, such as New York, Boston, Chicago, Washington, D.C., and San Francisco. Unlike video-dating services, these matchmakers—who probably number under a half dozen—personally interview clients and recommend potential dates based on the particular tastes and needs of the client. They charge hefty fees, ranging from $1,000 to $5,500. Most also conduct exhaustive national searches at the request of men and women with very specific requirements, and these can cost up to $30,000.

Abby Hirsch, the grande dame of matchmakers who founded The Godmothers about ten years ago, began by charging clients $250 for a minimum of three dates. She now charges $1,000 for five introductions and two evening seminars, and she has about one thousand clients on her roster in New York City and Washington, D.C., where, she claims, male clients outnumber females. "More women call, but they tend to be window-shoppers," she says. "Men who call usually sign up and they are more serious. Some come in because they want marriage; others want companionship; others want to fail. There's no guarantee you'll find someone, but we'll put you in touch with people who are compatible."

She says that 30 percent of the people who meet through her service form some kind of a dating relationship. "We've had in excess of four hundred marriages and only one divorce since we started. But people who have too many axes to grind, or who are too fussy, or unrealistic are likely to be in trouble. We also reject women who are really overweight, since men won't take them out, and we won't take men over fifty who want to take out much younger women. Men nowadays seem to want long-term partners, and more seem to talk about marriage without choking. They want women who aren't too angry or burned out, who are slender and athletic and pretty, and who are willing to make commitments. They want someone to talk to and trust; they want the security and the commitment; it's the difference between buying and renting."

But Abby is up-front about the fact that women in their forties outnumber men in their forties and fifties. Other matchmakers say that men and women sign up with different intentions. Women often come with a feeling that they have reached the end of the line, whereas men are often looking for a fantasy mate.

"The women who come to me are often in desperate straits. They feel they've lost out and are often yearning to have a child. They are lonely and want a good man," admits the head of a high-priced matchmaking service who demanded anonymity in exchange for being interviewed. "The men who come to me are so busy or fussy that they want the most beautiful women in the world and they often have a list of specific physical attributes. They're so accustomed to using consultants in every aspect of their lives that it feels natural to them to use someone else to help them find a marriage partner."

She also says that many men who use her service now want women who are not too career oriented. "Most men in their forties and fifties are less concerned with a woman's education than they were a few years back. They are turning to women who are more traditional. Women lawyers are the least favored by them, because they are so competitive. Men tend to want women who are working in fields such as interior design, teaching, and writing, because the women will be available to them and will be traditional wives. Women, on the other hand, don't want CPAs, actuaries, and engineers, because these men are perceived as nerdy."

She charges $5,000 for one year of service and she also conducts specialized national searches for a fee of $25,000 or more, most of them requested by men in their twenties who put her in charge of recruiting their dream woman.

She is quick to admit that she doesn't always have the right people on her roster. She does not restrict herself to men and women in her service when she is conducting a search, and she tends to act as a consultant as well as a matchmaker. She helps clients design and place Personals ads; she screens the people who answer the ads; and she mines her own network of clients and acquaintances to find appropriate partners.

When she receives a $25,000 assignment to conduct

a nationwide search, she may even go to modeling agencies to find a woman who fits her client's physical requirements. She also advises her clients about the dos and don'ts of courting, and she may intervene when a promising relationship hits a snag. "The least-motivated people are those who answer ads," she says. "The second most motivated people are those who place ads, and the most motivated people of all are those who go to dating services."

The real problem with high-priced matchmakers is that some of them are more interested in making money than matches. Helena Amran, a high-powered matchmaker who claims to have engineered over seven thousand marriages, generates $3 million a year in revenue from her New York office. She also has smaller branches in New Jersey, Israel, and England. Born and reared in Israel, Helena is an aggressive and public-relations-minded businesswoman who has been written up in many respectable magazines and newspapers as the guru of the dating world.

Helena charges a steep $5,500 fee to clients and invests heavily in ads, which appear regularly in major magazines and newspapers. When I began my research, I visited Helena—partly to see how she operates and partly to see if she could really find the man of my dreams. As I sat in a pleasant waiting room, I was asked to view a tape showing how her service worked and fill out an extensive biographical form. Then a counselor interviewed me. She told me that Helena conducts exhaustive psychological and background checks on all the men she recruits, to verify their biographical data, their marital status, and their earnings. She also requires AIDS tests.

When I asked to see some sample biographies of male clients, she declined. After all, I argued, I could find ordinary men on my own. If I was going to pay

$5,500, I wanted assurance that I was going to meet extraordinary men I couldn't meet at parties or through friends. She said that if I believed in the process, it would work. When I pressed the point, she admitted that if there weren't enough men for all the women who signed up, the agency would recruit them. When men were recruited, they didn't pay a fee. When I told several male friends about my experience, they told me that they had received calls from her counselors urging them to come in and use her service. They all thought that these calls were prompted by their answers to "real" ads in *New York*.

One man declined and had to be rude to get the counselor off the phone. Two others went to the office. One was turned off by the form, which required him to fill out a great deal of confidential information. He left before Helena could deliver her sales pitch. The other man stayed and was invited to scan her books of women and call them—free of charge—without any further investigation or screening. The only thing she requested was an AIDS test.

As far as I'm concerned, Helena is a fraud who has learned to prey on the vulnerabilities of women who are gullible and needy. She doesn't really screen the men she recruits; she won't tell women clients how she finds them; and she doesn't have enough men on her rosters to provide dates for female clients.

Apparently my suspicions were well grounded. Last spring Helena was sued by the Attorney General of New York State for overcharging clients and not providing them with dates. As this book goes to press, the case is still in litigation.[3]

The world of organized dating, like the world of organized crime, has become a hunting ground for money-minded entrepreneurs who have discovered that women are sitting ducks for all kinds of shams and scams that play to their needs and sensitivities. Yet when women don't get what they pay for—or when they meet sexual deviants through these services—they are usually too embarrassed to complain to legal authorities or sue the agencies.

Before you hand over several thousand dollars to a matchmaker, be sure to ask questions, just as you would ask questions if you were buying a car or an expensive mink coat. Insist on seeing some sample profiles of men. Insist on talking with other clients. Make certain you can get your money back if the matchmaker doesn't honor the terms of your agreement.

Singles Clubs and Mixers: Chaos or Conquest?

Social clubs that are sponsored by churches, synagogues, political parties, and charities are probably the safest—and still the most reliable—way of meeting other single people in a legitimate and enjoyable manner. Clubs that are organized around special interests, such as wilderness treks, tennis tournaments, bridge games, and gourmet dining, are also likely to be successful because it's easier to meet a man when you're enjoying a common activity than if you're simply standing around in a crowded room trying to make small talk.

When I was in my thirties, I decided to organize a social club with a few alumnae from my alma mater, Barnard College. We began by setting up a Christmas party for unmarried graduates of Barnard and Columbia colleges. (Both are part of Columbia University.) We rented a room in a local hotel and hired a band. Then we spent many evenings hand-addressing invitations to unmarried alumnae from Barnard who were thirty to forty years of age. With the help of the Columbia College Alumni office, we sent blind mailings to their alumni who had graduated in similar years and lived in New York City. (We couldn't distinguish married men from divorced or single men, so we sent out invitations to everyone, specifying that we were having a party for unmarried alumni.)

Two hundred men and women showed up at our dance, and in the course of the evening we recruited several graduates from Columbia College to join our committee. Then we organized a Valentine's Day party and invited all the people who had attended our first party. We sent another blind mailing to graduates of Columbia Law School and Medical School and we asked alumnae clubs from Smith, Vassar, and Wellesley colleges to invite their unmarried members in the appropriate age range. We allowed everyone to bring one friend and charged a nominal fee at the door to cover expenses and set up an operating kitty.

Our second party was an even greater success, and we decided to incorporate as an independent alumni organization, the Barnard/Columbia Alumni Social Committee Inc. We were informally sponsored by the university and we kept them informed of all our activities. We continued to hold either a lecture, a mixer, a tennis party, a skating party, a dance, or a museum event about every six weeks. We were rigid about attendees and would only admit people who received invitations or who were Columbia University graduates. We also allowed all invitees to bring one guest with them.

Within a short time we were sought out by single people who heard about us through word of mouth. At one point we hired a bouncer to keep intruders out. We were strictly nonprofit and made yearly donations to Barnard and Columbia.

Eventually I arranged a lecture at the Harvard Club, which featured Margaret Mead, a Barnard graduate and Columbia faculty member, who often lectured to university-based groups. She talked on "Singles: Past and Present." A few days before the event I sent a simple note to *The New York Times* asking them to cover the event, and much to my surprise they did. Two days later a handsome feature article appeared describing us as "the most intellectual singles club" in New York City.[4]

After the article, we received over two hundred letters from single people wanting to attend our events. Some sent lengthy resumes to see if their alma maters and professional expertise would make them eligible. We continued to set up more lectures with illustrious New Yorkers—the theatrical producer Joseph Papp, former Mayor John Lindsay, the writer Erica Jong (a Barnard graduate), the film critic Vincent Canby, Liv Ullmann, and the food critic Mimi Sheraton—all of whom agreed to speak for a small honorarium because we were a nonprofit group.

Eventually we grew into an organization with a list of over two thousand people on our roster. We were never a membership club because we didn't charge annual dues. We managed to cover our expenses by charging a small entry fee at the door, and we continued to monitor the people who attended our events.

As the president of this group for eight years, I learned that the essence of organizing a successful social club is setting up interesting events and maintaining an even balance of men and women. (When women began to swell our lists, we screened out those who weren't graduates of Barnard or Columbia University.)

We didn't want to make money—neither I nor any of the committee members ever received a dime for our labors—we simply wanted to have a good time and meet people in our peer group. And even though our ostensible purpose was to find dates, the real benefit of the group was developing a larger social network. I've gone into some detail about how this group was formed because I'm sure that any man or woman in any city can set up a similar social organization. There are alumni clubs in every city, and you can ask them to participate, either informally or officially. In smaller cities where there may be fewer alumni from any one college, you can set up an umbrella organization for alumni of several colleges.

You can also work with local community groups, Y's, churches, or even corporations. (We used to post invitations on employee bulletin boards of various hospitals in New York City.) It's easy to sponsor lectures enlisting speakers from local universities, who will talk about politics, money management, or relationships. Or you can organize tennis parties, walking tours, hikes, card games, ski outings, cooking classes —and just plain parties.

Most social clubs that succeed do so because they are guided by a motivated leader or group of people who will use some ingenuity—and a lot of hard work—to do the job. In retrospect, I dated only a handful of men I met through my organization, but I developed many friendships that have endured. For many years it was a focal point in my life and helped alleviate the isolation and alienation that are so often the downside of living in a large metropolis where social networking takes some effort.

The Singles Shopper: Why It Works

Shopping is not for everyone. A lot of women prefer to go about their business and let nature take its course. Given my druthers, I'd rather meet a man through friends or private small parties or simply through my work. And often I do. But I can't count on these sources to fuel my social life. (I've interviewed Robert Redford, Gregory Peck, and several CEO's. But they were all married at the time.)

So from time to time I either mine the Personals or sign up for a tennis party because I want to keep a flow of men in my life. I like the feeling that my social destiny is not completely in the hands of a chancy fate. It gives me some sense of control over my own life.

It also seems to me that whenever I really decide to meet someone, I do. About two years ago, when I was starting to work on this book, I made up my mind to meet a man. I answered about twenty-five ads in *New York*, enclosing a photo of myself that was reasonably flattering, and I placed an ad as well. Since it was the Christmas season, I also called up every organization I knew of that was connected with my profession and got myself invited to their holiday receptions.

As a result it seemed that I went out with a different man every night for a month. Some were real jerks. Some broke dates, but it didn't matter. I was so busy going out, I didn't have time to feel sorry for myself. I was in the driver's seat. When I finally decided to date a man I met through an ad on a steady basis, I wound up refusing a lot of other men, who kept on calling because I had kept them on a string.

Men seem to be turned on by women who are active and not readily available. In my view the real value of meeting a lot of men is that it blunts the feelings of loneliness that often develop when there's no man around. You wind up making yourself more desirable because you're busy and energized.

"I genuinely believe that there's not a closed market for anyone—I think it's a matter of finding people," maintains marketing executive Jim Blue. "I know women who have been extremely creative about meeting men—it's about who you are and where you go. There are a lot of places where businessmen dine; there are health clubs where men go. If you put yourself in a nontraditional environment, you can meet someone. If you can be truly honest with yourself about what you are looking for, there are ways to find that kind of man. If your attitude is that you can do it—you can find someone—that's more than half the battle. When I approach a job or a project and I have a positive attitude that it's going to happen, I have more success. And when I was single and wasn't emotionally involved, I found it was nice just to go out on a date."

SEVEN

Saying "I Do" Again: After Years of Solo Living

There's a common notion that divorced women have an easier time finding spouses than single women do because they have fewer fears of bonding—and greater fears of living on their own. Statistics show that a divorced woman *of any age* is more likely to marry than a single woman who is her peer: Marriage rates for divorced women are two to three times higher than those for single women. One-third of all recent brides were married previously. Almost one-half of these brides were thirty-five or older.[1]

"Divorced women have had the experience of living with a man," points out Martin Sylvester, a psychoanalyst and associate professor of social work at New York University. "They've often raised children and managed a household; they tend to be more accom-modating to men than single women, and they have a higher tolerance for idiosyncrasies. Divorced men may be attracted to them because they want women who will listen to them and be concerned and do tan-gible things, like fix dinner. Single women often ex-pect more attention from a man; they expect to be treated differently."

Other therapists point out that divorced women don't have the same fears of merging with a man that may inhibit single women from marrying. "Divorced women may be fearful of getting into the same situ-ation again, particularly if they've had a rough di-vorce," says therapist Robin Ashman. "They may fear losing their freedom and self-determination, but they don't fear intimacy. They've either resolved the issue or they never had it."

In fact many divorced women who remarry do so quickly, and younger women remarry faster than older women. In 1987 almost half of the divorced women in their early twenties who remarried had been divorced a year or less; a quarter of the women in their thirties who remarried did so within a year; and a fifth of women in their early forties who rewed also found spouses within a year of their divorce.

Therapists point out that the fear of loneliness is often the incentive that propels divorced women into speedy unions with the first receptive man they meet. "When a woman comes out of a divorce she is used to having someone living with her, and the pain of the loss may lead her to actively seek a partner," says Dr. Janice Lieberman. "If she's needy enough, she'll track a man down. Some of these women marry men who present even worse problems than their former mates. They never learned how to be independent in their first marriage or in the transition period after."

Many divorced women have serious financial pressures as well, since they are often shortchanged in
divorce settlements; if they have children, their burdens are more severe. Many don't have the skills and
experience needed to get good jobs. When they do
find work, they have to cope with double burdens.
Finding a husband as quickly as possible seems to be
the only way to survive.

"I was terrified of being alone, of finances, and of
managing money. I wanted someone to bear the burdens with me," said a divorced mother in her early
forties, who found a man to marry nine months after
she was separated. "I wanted to be married. I probably
would have gotten over the fear of living on my own,
but I never had to."

Hasty remarriages are probably one reason so many
second marriages fall apart. But not all women take
this path. Age either inhibits a woman's ability to remarry quickly—or it makes her more capable of
standing on her own two feet. Census data show that
the older a woman is when her marriage ends, the
more time she will spend shifting for herself between
marriages: In 1987, 20 percent of the women in their
early forties who remarried had been divorced nine
years or more; 30 percent of the women in their early
fifties who remarried had been divorced nine years
or more.

The male shortage is one reason for this pattern.
It's tougher for older women to find suitable husbands
than for younger women. Women with children are
more handicapped than women without children.
And many women emerge from marriages with so
many scars that they avoid men completely. It may
take them many years to trust men again.

But there are positive factors as well that influence
women to refrain from remarrying quickly. Almost

all the women I interviewed were divorced for an unusually long period of time—eight to eighteen years—before they remarried. Most of these women said they didn't want to remarry right away. They wanted time to rebuild their lives, take care of their children, and find their own way in the world before they even thought about looking for a new spouse. Some were free from the financial pressures that often impel women to seek husbands precipitously.

One divorced mother explained it this way: "I didn't need help financially, so I didn't feel any pressure to remarry. I didn't date for the sake of dating and was selective about accepting invitations. I was totally absorbed in my career and raising my children. I didn't want to take on a man with children of his own or a man with problems."

The critical issue is not *when* you remarry but *why* you remarry and *whom* you select as a spouse. If you remarry because you're afraid to live on your own, or because you're fearful that age will do you in if you wait too long, you may repeat the same mistakes that led to the breakup of your first marriage. If you give yourself time to know who you are and what you want and what you can offer a spouse, your chances of creating a solid marriage are enhanced.

When Children Fly the Coop

One critical factor that makes it more difficult for divorced women to marry than single women is the presence of children at home. The Wisconsin report shows that the more children a woman has, the less likely it is that she will remarry. One-quarter of the women with one or two children don't remarry; two-

fifths of the women with three children or more don't
rewed.[2]

The negative stresses set up by children are clear.
They demand time and energy and compound the
practical problems of developing a social life. When
suitors appear, some children become surly or unhappy because they don't want to share their mother's
love. In fact divorced men may be attracted to divorced mothers because these men miss the comforts
and tumults of family life. Single men may seek divorced mothers because they want a ready-made nest.
Other men are turned off. Either they don't want to
compete with children for a woman's love or they
don't want to take on a stepparenting role.

"The stepparent issue has to be traversed, and that
is complicated," says Dr. Janice Lieberman. "A mother
may feel that she is being disloyal to her children by
remarrying or that she is taking something away from
them. In addition, it's very difficult to establish a romantic relationship with a man when children are in
the house."

Children may also lessen a woman's incentive to
marry in more subtle ways: They provide satisfying
emotional connections and may dilute a woman's desire to develop a nurturing relationship with a man.
Divorced mothers may have fewer self-doubts about
their womanhood than women who don't have children and thus may have a less compelling need to
validate their femininity by the simple act of marrying.

But when children grow up and leave the house, a
woman's needs may change. "A woman may feel free
to pursue her own interests, or she may feel lonesome,
or she may seek a husband to once again take care of
someone," says Dr. Lieberman. "Even so, a divorced
woman who has formed an independent autonomous
personality will not take just anybody. She's apt to

make a sounder choice than a woman who remarries quickly after a divorce simply because she can't be alone."

War or Peace?

"Joel, my son, went to war when I began dating someone a lot," says Roberta Kappel, a forty-seven-year-old therapist and real estate entrepreneur with short, curly red hair, brown eyes, freckles, and an energetic personality who lives in Washington, D.C. "It's difficult when a boy has had his mother alone for some time. There's a powerful Oedipal dynamic at work," she states. "Joel set up so much stress that welcoming a new man into the house was like setting up a battlefield. So I tabled the idea of marriage while he was growing up."

Roberta met her first husband on a blind date. Stewart was tall, dark, and handsome, a well-to-do dental surgeon, forceful and assertive, the kind of man we used to call a "real catch." They married when Roberta was twenty-four and Stewart was thirty-one. "I was brought up to marry Stewart," Roberta recalls with a smile. "He was exactly the kind of man my mother wanted me to marry. He was extremely successful and aggressive; he always had to be in control. I was attracted to him because he was a star—and I wanted to be one myself. I thought marrying him would make me shine."

Their marriage was idyllic for a few years. They lived well and entertained frequently. When Roberta turned thirty, she gave birth to a son. Then things began to sour. Roberta began taking courses to develop a career as a therapist. She became tired of deferring to Stewart and his wishes all the time. Small arguments led to major battles. Three years later she insisted on a divorce.

"Stewart didn't like me studying because he wanted me to be available all the time," she recalls. "He was the superstar, and I was supposed to take care of him the way his mother did. I remember chairing a benefit and I was introduced as 'Mrs. Stewart Kappel.' I realized I could be known like that all my life and that no one would know the person inside. The marriage collapsed because I didn't keep up my end of the bargain. I wasn't what I promised to be when I married. I wanted to be a person in my own right, and Stewart didn't want me to change. He wanted me to play the game his way—and I refused."

Their separation was stormy, plagued by constant legal battles over money. Soon after, she met Alan, a separated father going through a tough divorce. He had a son about Joel's age. Roberta and Alan talked about marrying. Then Roberta began feeling more sure of herself. The more independent she became, the less she needed Alan.

"He wasn't right for me," she says. "At first I needed him because I was going through rough times. When I began feeling better about myself, we didn't like each other so much. He needed a dependent woman, and when I was no longer in terrible trouble, we didn't have much in common."

Joel was three at the time, and when she decided not to marry Alan, Joel was devastated. He'd formed close ties with Alan and his son. After that happened, Joel wouldn't trust any man who came into the house. He wanted his mother all to himself—and he got her.

As the years went by, Roberta adjusted to her situation and dated many men, but she kept them at a distance. "I don't tend to have light relationships, and the men in my life were here a lot," she recalls. "But they always left, usually due to explosions with my son. Joel got into fights with some of them. Other men got angry because I paid more attention to Joel. And I allowed them to leave because I didn't want to set up conflicts between Joel and myself."

She set up a practice as a therapist and developed a side business in real estate, a venture that made her feel more secure about her prowess as a money manager. Raising Joel also forced her to become self-sufficient. As she puts it, "If you have a sick child at three A.M. and have to go to work the next morning and don't have anyone to call, you become independent very fast."

Through the years Roberta cultivated a large and diverse circle of friends, and she frequently entertained. She was always on the go. "I'm active in my orientation," she says. "I tend to stir my own pots. I used to call men friends and ask them to find someone for me. And I fixed them up all the time."

When Roberta was forty-six, Joel went away to college. About that time a woman she had met in a study group introduced her to Barry, a fifty-eight-year-old lawyer who had been widowed for six years.

According to Roberta, Barry is not a "world-burner." He is a graduate of Harvard Law School, quiet and reserved, with a balding head and a slight paunch. He's not outwardly competitive, even though he is tops in his field as chief counsel for a major insurance company.

More important to her, Barry took care of his son, now twenty-five, and daughter, now twenty-two, through his wife's long bout with cancer. "There weren't a lot of fireworks at first," recalls Roberta. "We went out for a summer without much going on—I was very busy with my practice and dating someone else. But he was marriage-minded from the beginning, and that helped break down my resistance. He was also very persistent, and by the end of the summer I began to look at him differently."

They went to Mexico that fall, and Barry proposed. Roberta backed off. Even so, they continued dating and married nine months later.

"Barry's close to his kids; he's a hard worker; he's very generous and giving," she says. "He's a man I will live happily with rather than be bowled over by. He has a wonderful sense of humor, loyalty, and play. He comes from a happy marriage, and he likes me. He's not threatened if I'm not there when he comes home or because I have my own interests. I'm the one who runs around—and he likes my energy."

Her son is not euphoric about the marriage, but he accepts Barry and has not interfered or caused stress. "Joel says he's 'okay'—which is better than saying 'He's a jerk, Ma, get rid of him,' " says Roberta. "I've assured him that everything I have will go to him—his father has threatened to cut him out of his will."

Some people will say Roberta was lucky. She has a different take on the matter. "My theory of sexual relations," she says, "is that you have a taxi light on your head, and when it goes on, it hails others. Whenever I was open and wanted to find someone to date, I would find someone. When I met Barry, I was ready to get married and he came along."

The Stranger in Your Bed

The term *intimacy* has been bandied about so much that most people don't know what it means. Some of us still confuse intimacy with sex. Others define it as the sine qua non for marriage. Single men and women are often typecast as people who fear intimacy, simply because they've never married. The reality is that neither sex nor marriage is necessarily based on intimacy. Platonic friends can be more intimate than lovers or married people.

Erich Fromm and other modern therapists maintain that intimacy means revealing yourself fully to another person without the fear of being abandoned or criticized. It also means being accepting and making appropriate compromises when a lover reveals his or her vulnerabilities and needs.[3]

When people marry and are not self-confident, they may have trouble forming a truly intimate relationship because they are afraid to communicate their fears and desires. Their need for approval makes them so frightened of rejection that they are reluctant to open up, negotiate, and get—or give—what they truly want.

When a marriage collapses because the spouses do not communicate, a woman—or man—may unconsciously repeat the pattern of seeking unresponsive lovers, because it's the only pattern he or she knows. Such people are often afraid to get involved in another committed relationship because their first marriage was unhappy. Nor do they have the ability or self-confidence to reveal themselves and develop an intimate relationship. Instead they become involved in a series of affairs with unavailable partners. And this pattern continues until it becomes too painful—or until they gain enough self-confidence to end it.

"I Didn't Deserve a Reliable Man"

"After my divorce I didn't want to remarry," says Kathy Kirkland, a forty-five-year-old mother and administrative assistant with shoulder-length brown hair, a solid build, and a pleasant face. "So I chose men who weren't suitable, men who didn't want to get married. I wanted independence, and the price I paid was finding men who were unstable and unfaithful."

Kathy grew up in the Midwest, and after she graduated from college, she settled in Los Angeles to work in the entertainment industry. Soon after she arrived, she went to a party and met Tom, a talented and exciting screenwriter. They married when she was twenty-three and he was thirty-one. "I was scared of being alone," she recalls, "so I fell into marriage. It was the thing to do. We seemed to be in love. I wanted to have a baby."

Two years later she had a daughter and the marriage began to unravel. "We didn't have much money, and neither of us were really suited for marriage," she recalls. "Then we went off to Boston for a year, and Tom got involved with an actress. I was bitter and really began to dislike him. But in a way I was glad it happened because it provided a way out. I decided I wanted to live alone and raise my daughter and work."

When she turned thirty, they divorced. Kathy got a job as a secretary in a major film company just to pay the bills. There she met—and dated—men who were carbon copies of her husband. They were artistic, creative, charismatic, and unfaithful. "I dated a lot," she recalls. "And I was pretty wild. You build up a what-the-hell attitude after you've been married and through the hard knocks. But I wasn't promiscuous. I was responsible as a mother. I just wanted to have fun, so I selected men who were exciting. Most of them weren't willing to be faithful. And I wasn't sure I wanted them to be, because I didn't want to marry them. I felt I couldn't ask for a commitment if I wasn't ready to make one. In retrospect I think it's because I didn't have enough self-confidence to develop a close relationship. I was afraid to trust a man, partly because I didn't trust myself."

When she began dating Eddie, a well-known jazz musician, she changed her tune. They dated for three years and lived together for four more years. "I really wanted him to be faithful, and he refused," she says. "It drove me crazy. I wanted to kill him and started seeing a therapist to work it out. I felt torn because I wanted something I couldn't have—yet I didn't want to commit myself completely. We really weren't well suited; he was brilliant about music but cut off from the world and not expansive. I was in a trap and miserable."

She finally ended the relationship when it became too painful to continue it. She was forty at the time. Several months later she lost her job. She was feeling down and called Andy, a friend, to console her.

Andy was a film producer eight years younger than Kathy. She had met him five years earlier when he had shown up to work on a project with her boss. He was married at the time, so Kathy didn't see him as a romantic companion. But he came into the office frequently, and they became good friends. They were both unguarded because romance wasn't an issue. They talked on the phone almost daily about their problems and feelings. They met frequently for lunch.

When Kathy called Andy, he told her he'd just split up with his wife. They made a date for lunch. When she walked into the restaurant, she was unprepared for her reaction. "I'd met Andy in restaurants hundreds of times, and suddenly there was an aura of light around his head," she recalls with a smile. "I guess it was because we were both unattached. I went into the ladies' room and found myself unbuttoning the top button of my blouse and doing my hair, and I thought, What am I doing? This is my friend. But things were different."

A week later they went to a party and he dropped her off in a cab. She was disappointed because she wanted to stay with him. The next week he invited her to his apartment for dinner. She decided she would stay over, but she had to make the first move. "Andy was scared that I would say no. He didn't want to lose a good friend," she recalls. "That was smart on his part, because I had to make a statement before he did. He's the only man I ever dated who became a solid friend before we became lovers. If you can do it, it's the best way in the world to work it. By the time our relationship became sexual, we were really in love. But it didn't have the kind of sexual energy that knocks your socks off—the awful tension that used to come about with men who weren't there for me."

They dated steadily and eventually she found a new job. She moved in with Andy a year later, just after her daughter turned nineteen. They married when she was forty-four and Andy was thirty-six. "We enjoy the same things," she says. "We like taking long walks, Mexican food, and the same kind of humor. It's very comfortable. He's also volatile, and it took me a long time to get used to his anger. He's had panic attacks, and I've had to hold him up. He likes me because I'm very centered. He admires the fact that I've raised a daughter. And he would do absolutely anything for me. Even if I were completely disfigured, I know that he wouldn't leave me—he would be a brick. I've never had that with anyone."

Ditched in Midlife

Therapists say that when a divorce occurs after many years of married life, it's often the man who triggers the separation. "In a long-term marriage, it's usually the men who precipitate the breakup," says Roberta Jaeger, a training analyst at Columbia University School of Physicians and Surgeons. "Generally there have been years of unhappiness and difficulty, and men don't tolerate feelings of discomfort easily. They feel that if they change the situation—or their spouse—they'll change themselves. Women more easily accept limitations and bonds of loyalty, and they are counseled by parents and friends not to leave. Men don't get that kind of counseling from friends or even relatives. They feel they've missed something, and they'll look outside the home for another woman—and it's not as easy today to sustain a double life, since women won't put up with it."

On a trip to Chicago I met a divorced woman at the home of a friend. She is a highly competent bank executive and the mother of two grown children. Her husband had left her for another woman ten years before. She was overweight and dressed in sloppy cotton pants and a white T-shirt; her hair was messy and she wore no makeup. When we got into a talk about men, she became belligerent. "I don't believe in packaging," she told me and my hostess; both of us were wearing snappy new outfits. "Any man who wants me will have to take me as I am. What you see is what you get."

Not all women take that route.

◆

Anne Marie Okun, a tall, buxom blonde with an outgoing personality, set out on a different path when her husband took up with another lover after twenty-four years of married life. Anne Marie grew up in a Quaker family in Iowa. In high school she was very shy and had close ties to her mother and sister. When she was seventeen, she met Don. He was spirited and witty—a year older than Anne Marie. They married two years later. By the time Anne Marie was twenty-six, she had four children, two natural daughters and two adopted sons.

"I was attracted to Don because of his sense of humor and his wacky personality," she recalls. "I didn't realize there was a flip side that was hell to live with. I was a tagalong wherever we went. He was the life of the party. He was also controlling and verbally abusive; he said I could never do anything right. I got stomachaches when he blew up at me. But he didn't smoke or drink, and he had a good job. I wasn't brought up to get divorced—so we didn't. He kept his unhappiness to himself, except when he yelled at me for not being better."

When she was forty-two, Don moved the family from Portland, Oregon, to Kansas City, because he had a better job offer there. Anne Marie didn't want to go, but Don insisted. Three months later she was still unhappy, the children were cranky about the adjustment, and even Don was tense and somber. "Finally I asked him, 'What's wrong?'" recalls Anne Marie. "After all I was the one who was supposed to be unhappy: I left a job I liked, the kids missed their friends, and we were living in a rented house. But Don was getting more and more depressed every day."

They were taking a walk in the country and Don turned to her with a rueful gaze. "I left someone I loved in Portland."

"I started thinking of all the women I knew," she says. "I was in a state of shock when he said, 'It's not a woman, it's Fred.' "

Fred was Don's partner, a married man in his twenties who had worked with Don and looked up to him. "Don had been leading a double life, and I'm not even sure it was physical," she says. "He told me he'd always felt that way but had never acted on it until he met Fred. We went to a marriage counselor, and Don said he really wanted to stay married and fool around with men. I said, 'No way,' and sued for a divorce."

After their divorce Don moved to Milwaukee, where he set up housekeeping with his mirror image, a divorced man who was the father of four children.

Anne Marie didn't go out for a year. "I went to a therapist because I didn't want to come out crazy," she says. "I knew logically it wasn't my fault, but I kept asking myself, 'How could I not have known?' My therapist said I couldn't know if Don chose to keep it inside. But I felt stupid and betrayed. I needed to go through a period of grief and healing, and that's the most painful part—the time when the dream really dies and you know it's over."

She spent her days working and went to her health club every night. "I would run around the track wearing head tapes, and tears would be streaming down my face," she recalls. "Then I'd go home, get dinner, go to bed, and sob. I could take care of the boys—

the girls were in college—but I wasn't very supportive, and the youngest one took that on himself. He tried to take care of me."

Toward the end of the year she went to St. Croix with married friends. They met a bachelor there and became a foursome, playing tennis and eating dinner together under the stars. "It was fun and romantic, and I began feeling as though I was attractive enough to date again," she says. "That was the turning point."

When she returned to Kansas City, she joined a singles organization that sponsored tennis matches, ski trips, bridge games, and dances. She put an ad in a Personals column and answered ads as well.

"I'm fairly cheerful and friendly," she says matter-of-factly. "It was real easy to date, and I had a wonderful time. Despite my marriage I always felt confident about my sexuality and didn't have any problems about sleeping—or not sleeping—with men."

A year later she went back to college to finish her undergraduate degree because she wanted to enter law school. She also decided to remarry and began looking at all the men she dated as potential spouses. "I wanted a good, healthy man and didn't get involved with anyone I couldn't live with," she recalls.

One Saturday morning she was playing tennis in a round robin and met John. He was in his early fifties, a divorced father, who had one son living with him. He worked as an executive with a local bank. John called her as soon as she got home. "We started going out immediately, but he didn't really press to have sex for about six weeks," she says. "I felt that was nice because it showed he was really interested in me—and then we had to go to a hotel. Both of us had children at home.

"I realized he was a keeper right away, and I decided I could live with him. He's methodical, stable, and supportive of my law school studies. He doesn't have a temper."

John's reserved exterior had worked against him in his first marriage, which lasted sixteen years. He and his wife had never really communicated, and she finally left him to pursue her passion—playing bridge. She remarried a card shark and divorced again. John got custody of his son; his two daughters stayed with his ex-wife. His oldest daughter was deaf and not keenly aware of her mother's problems. His other daughter was desperately unhappy and tried to commit suicide. She went to a mental hospital for treatment and was released a year later, shortly before Anne Marie began dating John. Two months later his daughter attempted suicide again. This time she succeeded. "It was awful," recalls Anne Marie. "But it wound up bringing us closer because John had to start expressing feelings. He'd never had to do that before, partly because he grew up in a family where he wasn't encouraged to open up. I had to press him to talk about how he felt—and we still work on that."

When they married a year later, she was forty-four. "You don't look for the perfect person, because he doesn't exist," she says, summing up. "You look for the person who has flaws that you can live with."

◆

When women are abandoned by their husbands, many turn their anger inward and blame themselves. They often need a long period of time to recover—anywhere from six months to several years. When men are abandoned by their wives, they rarely mourn.

"When a woman rejects a man, it's a devastating blow to his manhood, but he doesn't feel he's failed her," says Martin Sylvester. "He becomes angry because he feels that she has not appreciated what he has done for her, and he usually runs around finding other women to console him—and he can easily find them. A woman feels abandoned and depressed when her husband deserts her," he continues. "She has the feeling she's lost out in a competition. She feels there's something wrong with her and that she has failed. Some women go to bed with every man they meet to prove they are still desirable sexually; others withdraw completely so as not to risk another rejection. But as they begin to feel more integrated, they begin seeking another man and another kind of life. Many look for a career or a second career as a way of establishing their own self-esteem."

Women like Anne Marie are able to establish a new life because their basic self-esteem is intact. They have been shattered, but not destroyed. Other women may have a tougher time recovering because they don't have as many internal or external resources to draw on. When you are abandoned by a husband and don't have a job, a circle of friends, or children at home to ease the blow, the journey will be more difficult.

Bouncing Back

"I was the last to know," recalls Amy Barrister, a tall, articulate blonde in her mid-fifties who divorced at forty-six and remarried at fifty-four.

"It's the old story—with a twist," she recalls with cynical amusement. "Richard was very proper and didn't want his image tarnished in any way. So he moved us all from Tulsa to Dallas to take a new job;

then he moved out of the house because he said he needed space—he'd devoted his whole life to me and our children and he wanted time to be on his own. I went along because I thought he was going through male menopause."

After he moved out, Amy went to Tulsa and called Nancy, her best friend and the godmother of her daughter, because Nancy was getting divorced. Nancy refused to see her, but Bill, Nancy's husband, invited Amy to lunch. Bill ordered a drink and then looked at Amy. "What do you think about Richard and Nancy?"

"What do you mean?" Amy asked.

"Don't you know? Everyone else does. They've been having an affair for the last two years."

Amy married Richard when she was twenty-two. It was a typical old-fashioned marriage. Richard was a successful actuary; Amy raised three children and taught elementary school. They were involved in community activities and had lots of friends. Nancy and Bill were their favorite couple.

"I thought we were happy and I worked hard," says Amy. "I probably worked too hard. I should have let the marriage go, but I thought we were going through hard times, and all couples go through hard times. Now I realize there were signs those last years. Richard only wanted to go out with Bill and Nancy. He was grouchy and moody around the house, but he pepped up around them. He didn't think much of my teaching. He said I was wasting my time because I wasn't earning enough money. He was also dogmatic and controlling. Everything had to be his way, and since I depended on him for everything, I hung in."

Amy was forty-six when Richard moved out. Her three children were away at college; she was a stranger in a new city; and she couldn't get a job teaching. She decided to take a course in real estate and soon got a job with a local firm.

"For a year and a half, I didn't do anything but work very hard and go out with lady friends—women I met through my job and a community group for new residents," she says. "But I didn't have any desire to socialize when I was invited to parties or events. I would say yes and then back out at the last minute. I was lonely inside but I didn't trust men and didn't feel good about myself. One day I realized I hadn't laughed in a year and a half, and I had always laughed a lot. I knew the affair wasn't my fault, but I couldn't help feeling I'd failed. So I kept myself busy with work and friends."

Eventually she went to a meeting of Parents Without Partners and joined a singles group for people over forty. The men she met began asking her out. She accepted, but she was wary and fearful.

"At first dating was horrible, just horrible," she says. "The pickings were lean, and I went out with some men who were pleasant, others who were terrible. Sex was very difficult. I was a virgin when I married and hadn't known any other men in that way. I was very careful and only had sex with a few men. I was afraid to try and find out I wasn't appealing. So I never let myself get really involved. And it got to be a joke— a lot of men stopped seeing me for that reason. But I had to know a man very well before I could go to bed with him."

For four years she dated one man who was eight years younger than she was, but not really compatible. She dated other men who became friends. She joined other community groups, and her real estate business began to thrive. "It became like a snowball going downhill, and each year was better and better," she says. "It was like my wildest dream come true, and that gave me a reason to feel positive about myself. Richard couldn't have handled my success—he would have liked the money, but he would have been too threatened."

Shortly after Amy turned fifty-two, she went to a restaurant to meet a woman friend for a drink. While she was waiting at the bar, a man next to her struck up a conversation. Alan was fifty-two, a twice-divorced marketing executive and the father of three children, all in his custody. A month after Alan met Amy, he invited her to dinner. "We had a pleasant time," she recalls, "but it wasn't any big thing at first. We continued dating, and I also kept on seeing other men because I was still wary of being really involved. That was my defense."

Ten months after they met, Alan proposed. "I was scared," admits Amy. "I had a fear that if I married again, the nice person I married would change. I couldn't go through another divorce. I told him I couldn't risk failing again. He said, 'Are you going to go through life being afraid to take a chance because one marriage failed? You've got to live your life— you've got to live each day—and if it fails, it fails. What if it succeeds? Do you want to miss out on that?' "

So Amy took the risk. "I'm different than I was ten years ago," she says, summing up. "I'm more independent and I've learned to stand up for myself. I take pride in what I do. Alan's happy, jolly, and fat —a real contrast to Richard, who was depressed a lot, and slim. Alan's also hotheaded and likes to run things. We've had trouble with that, because I've learned to do things for myself. But he's loving and caring and supportive of my work. We fight a lot about details, but we work them out. I never thought I'd be able to trust a man again, but I do."

Peer Relationships

Richard and Amy are a typical example of a traditional first marriage in which the husband is the primary provider and decision maker. When people from these marriages divorce and remarry, they often select spouses who are more equitable as partners. Men may welcome a woman who will be an equal earner, and women may seek out a man who will allow them to pursue their own careers.

We often think of these marriages as peer arrangements because the husband and wife each contribute financially to the marriage. This often dilutes the husband's power and gives the wife more leverage in shaping the relationship and making primary decisions. Psychologists, however, point out that income is not the real leveling agent in peer relationships.

"The balance of power in marriage is affected not only by income but also by a very central aspect of marriage: the traditional male-provider role," maintain Blumstein and Schwartz in their study on American couples. "When the husband believes in his provider role, he has the greater say in the important decisions. If his wife shares the same view, then she yields to his wishes. . . . Even if a wife earns a great deal of money—perhaps even more than her husband—she will not necessarily acquire a proportionate amount of power."[4]

Real peer relationships can only develop when a high level of commitment and trust exist within the marriage and partners are able to make decisions without using tactics that are manipulative or exploitative. That is why you can have a true peer relationship with a man who is much older—or much younger, or much more successful, or much less successful—than you are. If your income, age, and education are similar, they may enhance your ability to function as peers, but they do not create it. You can have an imbalanced relationship with a man who is exactly your own age and an equal earner if one of you is always angling for power or fearful of being rejected.

"Efforts to explain the bases of power, or why individuals perceive power in their relationships to be egalitarian or imbalanced, have focused on three sources: authority, comparative resources, and dependency," writes Elizabeth Grauerholz, a psychologist at Purdue University. "Interpersonal values such as trust, social orientations, or commitment have been largely ignored. Yet it is precisely these factors, unique to intimate relationships, that are likely to be related to perceptions of one's partner and interactions in the relationship, especially when power-based resources are relatively balanced. . . .

"Because trusting persons, by definition, feel that their partners would not hurt or exploit them, they may be unwilling to believe their partners are more powerful and thereby have the ability to exploit them. Consequently intimates who have built strong trust are likely to perceive the relationship as more egalitarian than those individuals who are less trusting of their partners."[5]

That is also why people with a high level of self-esteem are more likely to develop egalitarian relationships than people who are not self-confident. When a woman spends a long period of time on her own and is required to support herself and her children, she often develops the strength and self-confidence that many men admire, and the two of them often form a relationship that is truly egalitarian.

"I Refused to Become a Victim"

"I married the first time because I was absolutely and madly in love," recalls Janet Belton, a brunette with an outgoing personality, who fell in love with a classmate during her freshman year at a college in Manhattan. Janet was a music major; Stephen was a budding opera singer. They married two years later and had two children when they were in their early twenties.

When Stephen was thirty, he failed a critical audition at the Metropolitan Opera House. He then acted out his disappointment by having an affair with one of Janet's best friends. When Janet confronted him, Stephen moved in with the woman and her husband, a doctor who was involved in research and happy to have his wife off his hands.

"I was devastated, not only because she was my best friend, but because it was all done in such a Machiavellian way," recalls Janet. "He accused me of being paranoid."

A year later Stephen went to India to follow a guru. When he returned, he joined a Bhagwan Sri Rajneesh cult in Oregon and married a member. Then he returned to India and married yet another cult member.

Janet tried to get a legal separation, but Stephen wouldn't sign a binding agreement. Every time he appeared in court, he sabotaged the proceedings. "I couldn't deal with him—so I decided to assert myself right away," says Janet. "I knew I could wallow in my own depression, but I refused to become a victim. I had developed survival techniques because I grew up in a volatile family, and I put them to use."

Janet went to a therapist, joined a support group for divorced women, and began to upgrade her professional life. She became a full-time music teacher and eventually moved on to editorial work and fund-raising. She also began dating, but without any intention of remarrying. "It was important to be part of the world," she says. "But I was cautious and questioned my judgment of people. I was also upset and bitter, since I didn't have any financial support. I had to concentrate on survival for a long time."

Four years later Stephen influenced her two children to take drugs—they were twelve and thirteen at the time. Then he kidnapped them and took them to India for a year. Janet got them back only because he was arrested at the border for smuggling hashish out of India.

When her children returned, she focused on building a life-style in which she could be happy with—or without—a man. "I had an active social life and I never felt alone," she recalls. "I never felt I had to get married to be a complete person—I always had too much to do. I volunteered for music organizations and school activities; I read a lot; I went to the ballet and concerts; and I had a lot of male and female friends. I met people easily—I was chatty and easy to talk to."

As she earned more money, she felt she was on firmer ground. About the time she turned forty, she revised her goals. "I began to feel freer emotionally," she says. "I didn't go on a husband search, but I decided to look for a man who could be in a long-term and serious relationship."

Some months later she went to a dinner party to be introduced to a male friend of the hostess. Unexpectedly one of the couples brought a guest who was visiting from Concord, New Hampshire. Bill was a forty-three-year-old engineer, who had left his wife six months earlier, after twenty years of married life.

Janet and Bill hit it off right away and talked together in the living room while Janet's intended suitor sulked in the corner. Bill took her home and said he would call. "I thought, He won't—it's the old story. I'll never see him again. Besides, he's in Concord."

Bill called the next day. Three weeks later he visited her in New York. After that they began seeing each other every weekend; either he commuted or she did. A year later she moved to Concord to live with him. The next year they bought a house together. Two years later they married.

"I was very balanced when I met Bill," she says. "That was good for us because he was very vulnerable. His ex-wife was giving him a tough time about the children, and she also wanted me out of the picture. He needed a woman who was strong and patient.

"Within months I knew the relationship could lead somewhere. Bill was intelligent, adventuresome, fun to be with, and honest. He was also up-front about his fears and wary of marrying right away. For a while he was seeing another woman. I told him to fish or cut bait. I thought there was real potential, and the longer our relationship went on, the more problems we solved. Gradually I got him to let go of his feelings of guilt about his ex-wife, and he was always responsive when I brought up issues and took a stand. When I moved, I was willing to take the risk that we wouldn't get married. I knew it wouldn't destroy me if it didn't work out, so I took a chance. I got a job right away, and now I love it here. One of my friends says I'm like steel—very strong and very flexible."

♦

People who are insecure often try to compensate by being controlling and manipulative. In contrast, when you trust your own integrity, you can make reasonable demands that will help your partner grow. You can also respond to your partner's needs without feeling that you are being exploited. Real strength *is* like steel—it is supportive yet flexible.

These qualities are appealing to men as well as women—particularly if a man is emerging from an unhappy marriage. Women frequently say they appreciate men who are "there for them." Men also need women who are supportive. As Stanton Peele points out, mature love involves the ability to make demands—and receive demands—that enhance growth, awareness, and vitality. The more self-sufficient you are, the freer you will be to reject men who are rigid but not strong—and to be flexible yourself. "Mature people, concerned with the quality of their lives, engage naturally in a continuing evaluation of their relationships, testing alternatives and questioning their commitments," he writes. "An independent open person exploring life seriously will instinctively (if not consciously) consider whether someone has anything of substance to add to his or her existence."[6]

Widowed in Midlife

Contrary to the common view that few women are widowed before their late fifties or sixties, many women do lose husbands prematurely due to heart attacks, illness, and accidents. In 1985 a third of all widows were under the age of fifty when their husbands died.[7] Since many of these widows are solely in charge of raising their children, they often have a hard time finding new spouses who want to take on a full-time parenting role.

Widows, however, do have some psychological advantages. If their marriage was happy, they know what it's like to give and receive love. As a result they may not have the same problems with self-esteem that often undermine women who have been jilted by their husbands. Their main challenges may be practical rather than psychological: finding a husband who can replicate the one they lost; raising children on their own; earning money; and adapting to single life.

◆

"I never felt abandoned or rejected," says Mimi Sachs, a social worker in Cleveland whose husband died in his sleep from a heart attack. He was thirty-seven at the time; she was thirty-five. Their three children were nine, seven, and four. "I never felt entitled to happiness forever," recalls Mimi. "What wrenched me was watching my children suffer: One asked, 'Who is going to answer all my questions?' and another asked, 'Who is going to teach me chess?' They didn't know how their lives would continue, and I was helpless to take away their pain."

She didn't have time to feel sorry for herself or even mourn. Nor did she consider dating for six months. When she decided to look for men, she didn't know what to do. "I wasn't scared of marrying because I knew if I chose a man I could really respect, I would be okay. But I wasn't ready to deal with it. I needed time to find out who I was when I wasn't part of a team."

Mimi had married when she was twenty-four. When she began dating again, she felt awkward and uncomfortable. She didn't know the rules, but she was also needy. "My first date was a bomb," she recalls. "I remember having dinner and watching myself interact. I didn't know what to do or say. I had to date to prove I was alive—but I was using men unfairly because I wasn't ready for a relationship. I didn't know how to say no to someone—and I didn't know how to indicate I was interested."

A year later she hired a baby-sitter once a month so that she could go out to social events. "It had nothing to do with getting married," she says. "I had to make a statement that I was not helpless and could control my life. I went to singles parties, weekend outings, tennis nights, and I even tried a Personals ad. I wanted to prove that I could do something and wasn't feeling sorry for myself."

Because she had a good self-image, she wasn't upset if a man wasn't interested in her. "I didn't even have time to see my friends. Why should I spend time on men who couldn't give me what I needed?" she says. "I didn't need to prove that I was valuable by making a man like me."

She had three relationships during the next five years. She met two men at parties; a third was a friend of her first husband. All three had serious intentions, but they didn't suit her needs. "The toughest thing was saying no. I had to gamble that I wouldn't be alone."

When she was forty, friends arranged a dinner party to introduce her to a fifty-year-old widower who lived in a distant suburb. Bert's wife had died six months earlier after a long illness. He had four children, he was the same religion as Mimi, and he was an international businessman. "When he walked in, I remember thinking that he seemed to be solid and attractive," she says.

The next day he called her for a date. After several more dates they planned a picnic with all their children. "I couldn't visualize how to integrate seven kids—and pick up dinner for nine," she says with a laugh. "But Bert was good at managing, and the kids were cooperative. No one felt they had a right to make it not work."

Five months later they decided to think of themselves as a couple. "It was comfortable and nice," she recalls. "I could relax. It wasn't filled with trauma—there were no ups and downs—we could talk on a lot of different levels. He was clearly focused. He needed a woman who was good with kids and a best friend, a woman who could share his life and values. And I needed a man who could share my life and be a good father."

When Bert asked Mimi to marry him several months later, he insisted that she move to his town. "The kids were angry and felt that I didn't go to bat for them," she says. "But I knew I couldn't win that issue and decided the overall gain was greater than the loss.

"When you marry, you have to set priorities and figure out what's really important. Bert was in control of himself and responsible; he was active in the community; he was Jewish-oriented; he cared about his work and he was very affectionate.

"The toughest thing was saying yes. I had to gamble that someone else wouldn't come along. The irony is, I found out that I hadn't really changed: The man I selected the second time was the same type of man I selected when I married in my twenties, but I had needed space to explore and find out what I really wanted."

They married the following spring and renovated a house. Their main issues became dealing with seven children and making time for them all. "Bert as a new father wasn't an issue, but dealing with a new personality was," she says. "The kids liked the security he gave us and his directedness, but they felt he didn't listen enough and gave too many orders. They all got enough group time, but not enough individual time. They had to learn to negotiate with us, and they had to negotiate rights and power with their other siblings."

Eventually everyone learned to adjust. "They're all reasonably on track," says Mimi. "A few months after we married, my youngest son wrote in a school essay, 'When my father died, my mother set out to find a new father for us, and she found Bert Sachs. She set out to create a new family and she did it.' "

◆

Clearly, divorced or widowed women have a hard time finding good spouses. The male shortage is real. Children can set up unusual stresses. The past may leave deep scars. But if you are divorced you have the choice not to be angry forever. You have the choice to remember what was worthwhile in your first marriage and try to understand what went awry. You have the choice to blame yourself or to forgive yourself; to feel anger at your ex-husband or to let the anger go; to resent your children, or to love them.

If you choose to blame and keep your anger alive, you are sustaining the ties and bad feelings that will interfere with your ability to find a second spouse. Growing up means taking responsibility for your actions. It means learning from your mistakes and moving forward. It means trusting your ability to receive love—and give it—when you find someone worthy.

EIGHT

About Men: The Readiness Is All-Important

Most women who have been dating for a number of years have had unhappy experiences with men who were charming, sexy, successful—and were unwilling to sustain or develop a healthy relationship. As Guttentag and Secord point out, the male shortage is one basic reason for this pattern. In any situation where women outnumber men, men do not feel pressured to cement relationships quickly. They may want sex right away—and get it—but they don't want commitments right away. Men are also less likely to accommodate themselves to imperfect relationships, and they may move on when problems develop. It's easier for them to find another relationship than to compromise or work out difficulties.

On the other hand, when men do decide to marry,

they have an easier time finding spouses than women with a similar mind-set because they have a wider pool of potential partners. "It's a man's world in many ways," says Seymour Coopersmith, a Manhattan psychoanalyst who married for the first time in his mid-fifties. "Men who are relationship-prone find someone right away. If they're viable as partners, you have to find them before someone else does."

Gender conditioning also contributes to these patterns, according to psychologist Herb Goldberg. Women, he contends, define their femininity in terms of their ability to develop a loving relationship with a man. Many pressure men prematurely for commitments and closeness because they want to fill a need for emotional security and to validate their femininity. Often they want a commitment more than they want a specific man.

Men, in contrast, define their masculinity in terms of their ability to be autonomous, controlling, and sexually potent. Often they have trouble admitting that they want closeness with a woman because it challenges their need to be independent and in charge. When a woman presses a man for a commitment before he has developed strong feelings for her—or when she tries to control the relationship—he may react by creating distance or breaking away completely.

"Feminine pressure for commitment from a man in a relationship is the counterpart and equivalent to the traditional masculine pressuring of a woman for sex," writes Goldberg in *The Inner Male*. "Most women feel vulnerable when they have sex without commitment. Men feel equally vulnerable when there is early pressure for commitment. They get scared, just as women get scared when they are pressured for sex by a relative stranger."[1]

The ideal solution, he maintains, is for both partners to let go of their gender defenses and thereby enable a relationship to evolve naturally, so that commitment is the outcome of the relationship—and not the goal. But since sexual involvements usually occur before intimacy can possibly develop, women often have to do more accommodating than men. They have to restrain their impulses to force a commitment in exchange for sexual favors and focus instead on what is happening as the relationship does—or does not—progress.

"Women will be better able to understand men's obsession with sexuality when they grasp the irrational nature of their own obsession with commitment," writes Goldberg. "In an authentic, loving relationship the commitment is just there—a by-product, not an entity in itself—as in a best friendship. With a loving friend you want to be committed because you care about the person. . . . The trust and safety are there if it's a friendship built on genuine love and caring. A nondefensive relationship, like nondefensive sex, is a process that emerges from two people feeling safe and good about each other."[2]

A man who is truly ready for a committed and healthy relationship will treat you well and respond to your needs, just as he would respond to the needs of a valued friend. Conversely you will treat him as a man—and not an object—and give him the same consideration you would give a good friend. A climate of trust will develop spontaneously, without prodding and artificial promises.

It doesn't matter if a man has been separated for six months or divorced for fifteen years. His track record with other women is not the determining factor. What counts is how he treats you. Even diehard bachelors can marry, and so can men who have been divorced for many years. Roughly two-thirds of the men who remarry over the age of thirty-five do so within five years of their divorce. A third, however, remarry *any time* after that. In 1987, approximately 10 percent of the divorced men in their forties who remarried did so nine years or more after they had been divorced, and 16 percent of men in their fifties who remarried did so nine years or more after they had been divorced.

Men also go through cycles. Men change. We've all heard stories about bachelors who suddenly turn into family men and womanizers who wind up at the altar with women who are fat and frumpy. Sometimes the trigger is the death of a parent, a child maturing, a critical illness, or the sudden awareness of their own mortality. Sometimes the trigger involves interior changes that are hard to track or categorize. Many men, for example, decide to marry or remarry when they achieve success in their career—or realize they will never achieve their fantasy goals.

As Daniel Levinson points out, there's a growing turning "inward"—a decreasing emphasis on assertion and mastery and a tendency to enjoy the process of living rather than the attainment of specific goals. "External success and failure become less important as criteria for inner well-being," he writes. "The quality of [a man's] total life acquires greater significance than the quality of his success on any single dimension."[3]

"I Was Not Happy Single"

The reason so many men remarry quickly after a divorce is that they are unable to adjust to single living.

Many men won't even finalize a marital separation until they have found a new wife. That may be why almost 20 percent of men who remarry do so within six months of their legal divorce. "A man who has been married is accustomed to having a woman take care of things," says Martin Sylvester. "He has a deep motivation to find a new woman who will replace his wife and who will take care of the cooking, the shopping, and the social arrangements in his life. And because there are more women available than men, a man can usually find a new wife easily."

♦

Jim Black, a forty-eight-year-old marketing executive, is a trim, pleasant-looking man with glasses and brown hair. His first marriage lasted twenty years and was unhappy for a long time. He remarried four years after he was divorced. "There was never a question in my mind that I wanted to remarry," says Jim. "I was not happy being single. After visiting my children on weekends, I was miserable and would break down in tears in the car on the way home. I realized I could date a lot, but I didn't like the singles scene. I missed the stability and support system of married life. I'm a social animal and not a hermit."

Jim had married when he was twenty-three; his wife was twenty-one and pregnant. "I wasn't ready for marriage, but abortions weren't acceptable then," he says ruefully. "Marriage was the only thing to do."

Two years later they had another child. Jim's wife stayed home and cared for the children. Jim worked hard to support the family by taking high-paying jobs he didn't like. "If there hadn't been children, we probably would never have stayed together," he admits. "We were both classic avoiders. We never talked about our feelings; we never discussed anything other than who should take our children to the doctor. I developed a tremendous obligation to support the family which had nothing to do with what I wanted to do. My wife was always terrified that I would quit my job—she needed someone to take care of her. I was always miserable even though I adored the children and liked the stability of family life."

Their marriage finally collapsed when the stresses of not communicating became overwhelming. "I couldn't convey my anxiety to her, she couldn't convey her fears to me," he says. "Finally it became intolerable at home because we couldn't talk. I left because we weren't dealing with any issues."

Jim went to a therapist to work out his problems. He also tried to date, but he was so unhappy that he couldn't get involved with other women. A year and a half later he returned to his wife to work out a reconciliation. But it was a mistake. He and his wife lived in different rooms of their house and they each dated other people. Finally Jim's wife decided to sever the cord because the situation was so painful.

"I went through the crazies when we finally split," says Jim. "I was euphoric because I was away from the tension of not being talked to. I was also devastated about ending such a long marriage. But this time I didn't have as much of a problem adapting because I was already involved with another woman. Having someone made it easier to separate."

He lived with his new girlfriend for a year. When that ended, he met another woman and they lived together for almost a year. After his second relationship fell apart, he joined a dating service and answered Personals ads. He preferred organized channels because he was not aggressive about meeting women at parties or at bars.

"I realized there was a dearth of eligible men," he

recalls. "I could date without any problem at all. But most of the women I met were guarded because they'd been burned. I felt I was being scrutinized. If I said I really enjoyed being with them, they didn't trust what I said. I also went through a period where I wanted to get as many women as possible into bed, but that didn't last long. It was awful—and simply an ego trip. I never played women along. I told them what the score was."

About a year after his second relationship ended, he had a lunch meeting with a potential client, a strong-minded sales executive in her early forties. As soon as Jim met her, he thought she was the type of woman he could marry. Brenda had been married briefly in her twenties and she told Jim she was interested in remarrying, partly because she wanted to have a baby. Yet when Jim tried to develop a more substantial relationship with her, she backed off. For two months they met for dinner and didn't have a romantic involvement.

"She was dating someone else," says Jim, "and I was dating the world. But I always enjoyed seeing her. She didn't mince her words. She's very outgoing and bright, and her life is on her sleeve. I finally took a stand. I said, 'If you don't want to spend more time with me, forget it. I don't want an unavailable woman.'"

His ultimatum persuaded her to change course. She invited Jim to spend a weekend at her summer house. It was June. When they returned, Jim canceled the dates he had set up with other women. Two months later they decided to live together, and Jim proposed a month after that. They married that December, and within four months Brenda got pregnant. She was forty-three when she gave birth to her son.

"We decided jointly to have a baby and talked about it before we married," says Jim. "A child was very important to Brenda because she didn't have children, and that was fine with me. There's no question in my mind that I made the right decision.

"Does Brenda do things that drive me up the wall? Absolutely. Do I do things? Absolutely. We fight a lot. My first wife and I never fought, and that was part of our problem. Brenda is also different from my ex-wife because she doesn't have to be cared for as a child. She's got a good career and I don't feel the overwhelming burden I felt in my first marriage to provide. We do a lot of caring and sharing, and she's the right person for me. People who are single miss the benefits of bonding and having a trusting relationship."

The Candy-Store Syndrome

When men manage to transcend the feelings of loneliness that occur after a marriage dissolves and find that they can take care of themselves, many also discover that getting dates is as easy as buying a chocolate bar in a candy store. The only question is, What kind of chocolate do you want and how much do you want to spend?

Admittedly men who are good-looking, successful, and affluent are more sought out by women than men who are only moderately successful, good-looking, or affluent. But even these men tend to have an easy time, particularly if they are charming and pleasant.

Some of these men remain single for a number of

years, and the reason may be their inner conflicts about bonding. That is why some men are almost always available as dates and are so visible in the singles scene. Other men who resist marriage for a period of time may not have conflicts about intimacy. But many become hooked on the excitement of conquering new women—and leaving them—as soon as a relationship begins to assume a predictable pattern.

"Relationships often begin with an intense emotional experience that's invigorating," explains Arthur Parsons, chairman of the Department of Sociology and Anthropology at Smith College. "But when that intensity burns off, people who thrive on excitement find their interest waning and go on to find new partners. These same people may be very successful in corporate life, where there are short-lived but intense relationships and constant variety."

Eventually, however, these encounters may turn out to be draining, not stimulating, and then many men become receptive to women who want a stable relationship. Sometimes the spur is a fear of growing old and the knowledge that in their twilight years they won't be as attractive to young women. Sometimes the spur is simple fatigue. "A man can get to a point where he realizes it's now or never," says Seymour Coopersmith. "Regardless of the anxieties that exist, a man realizes that if he doesn't marry now, he probably never will. It's similar to a woman over forty who wants a baby—it becomes a question of finding a man whom she can have a baby with and not finding Mr. Perfect. Men also realize they don't have as many options to wait for a fantasy mate. What they need is a viable relationship with a woman who is comfortable and available to them."

"I'd Been Around Every Corner"

"I had learned what I had to learn; I knew what was around the corner—I'd been around enough corners to know that I didn't have to see any more," says David Sandler, forty-nine, an entertainment lawyer in Los Angeles with a warm, expansive personality.

"I lived out my fantasies and I stopped. I knew what it was like to screw a starlet, and I didn't have to find out anymore. I got tired of the stories and I just wanted to know someone well enough to say, 'Hey, bring a book over.'"

David married after he graduated from Harvard Law School. He was twenty-four. His wife was twenty and the homecoming queen of her college. "We married packages and essentially we played house. We didn't know who we were as people," he says. "She was beautiful and a folk singer. My family was ecstatic, and so were all my friends. She taught school and I decided to save the world. I got involved with civil rights. We had a baby three years later, but I never thought of myself as a father. I thought of myself as a son."

Then they had two more children, and David and his wife grew apart. "She was there but we weren't really together," he says. "She was passive in a lot of ways and afraid of the world, and she let me do everything. At first it didn't bother me that much because I didn't know what marriage was supposed to be."

Eventually his wife slid into a serious depression. David took a lot of the blame because he felt he wasn't in touch with her needs. "I thought we should try to work it out," he says. "But it became impossible because we simply weren't suited for each other. We were both alone."

They divorced when David was thirty-five. He lived on his own for the first time and dated a lot. "For a long time I was learning and doing what I should have been doing in my twenties," he says. "I went out with women of all ages and all types. And as I learned about myself, I realized that I liked women who were creative and independent. I shied away from women who called me all the time to tell me about their problems."

Several years later his wife remarried. David continued to enjoy his life as a bachelor and never felt pressured to marry—or not marry. Since he was an entertainment lawyer, he was frequently invited to film screenings, parties, and museum openings, and many women he met made overtures to him. If they didn't, he had no hesitation about approaching them.

But he didn't sustain relationships. "I don't know whether it was neurosis or laziness on my part, or if the women simply weren't the right ones," he says. "Sometimes, I just didn't love them enough. Even if they were pushing some buttons in me, they weren't pushing enough buttons to make me want to stay."

Then eight years after his divorce, a tragedy occurred that changed his life forever. His ex-wife was killed in a car crash.

"My life did a flip-flop," recalls David. "I suddenly became responsible for three children who were all traumatized by the death of their mother. I moved into a new house and I became responsible for them on a day-to-day basis. Things that used to upset me didn't even touch me I used to wake up at four A.M. with anxiety attacks. I always had to plan ahead. Dating was far down on the list of my priorities.

"Everyone thought I'd remarry quickly because

they saw me as vulnerable and needy. That scared me because I knew in my gut it would be a disaster if I married for the wrong reasons, so I became even more cautious about the women I dated. I didn't have the time to juggle anymore. I had to make decisions about women more quickly. I'd ask a lot of questions and, by the end of a drink, I'd know more about a woman than some men would know at the end of several weeks."

During his late forties, David's two eldest children went to college and his mind-set began to change. He decided to explore relationships fully instead of finding excuses to end them. He dated one woman for six months. When that began to wind down, he decided to call a woman producer who had been highly recommended by a friend. "That was another change, because I waited to call her until the relationship was almost over," says David. "Usually when I got such a high recommendation, I would call a new woman right away, even if I was dating someone else."

Sandy was thirty-six and single. She had shoulder-length brown curly hair and a sexy smile. "Sandy was creative and independent," says David. "She didn't make unreasonable demands on me. She could take care of herself when I went home to my kids. We dated steadily for six months. Then she told me, 'We've both been around a long time and we know enough after six months. Either we marry or we split. If we think about it too much, it will never happen. We can always find excuses not to.'

"I agreed with what she said," explains David. "But I knew there would be a lot of turmoil at home that she couldn't anticipate. She had never been married; her dreams were intact. I knew I was right, yet I loved her. How could I say that and make it sound as though it simply wasn't an excuse? So we went ahead. And it turned out to be right. Even though there was up-heaval at home, there was never upheaval about our underlying feelings for each other. This is where I am, and it's where I want to be. One hundred percent is when you are there and it's okay. It's when you can stay."

"I'm Black and Broke but I Can Cook"

Caring for young children is often the reason di-vorced women don't remarry quickly. It's less com-mon for men to be restrained due to child-rearing responsibilities, but men who take on a primary-pro-vider role can also be deterred. Some men can't afford to take on a new wife while they are financially re-sponsible for their children. Some don't want to bring a stepmother into the picture who will set up stress and resentment. Others are so involved in the actual process of caretaking that they don't actively look for a new spouse until their children are grown.

◆

"My sons always came first. I would spend a lot of time with them, and women wanted more money and time than I could give them," says Andrew Prentiss, a forty-nine-year-old black man, now the husband of Nancy Taylor.

Andrew grew up on the seamy South Side of Chi-cago; his parents divorced when he was six years old. As a youngster he hung out in poolhalls, where he interacted with druggies, dope dealers, and stick-up artists. He lived with his mother and spent summers in Arkansas with his grandmother.

"Mother taught me to stand up for what you believe," he recalls. "I lived by myself the majority of the time because she was working nights. That's how I learned to cook—I had to help her. My grandmother taught me that you don't put your feet under the table until you put your food on the table. Everyone had to put something in the pot."

During high school Andrew worked forty hours a week to support himself and his mother. After graduating he began working for an automotive company. Eventually he worked his way up to a position as a senior sales manager. When he was twenty-one, he married. He and his wife had two sons and divorced seven years later. "I don't know what attracted me to her," he says now. "She was dumb and she still is. There was no line of communication, and she spent too much time drinking and being high on drugs. I finally had to walk; I couldn't take it any longer."

From then on he spent all of his weekends with his boys and many weekdays as well. He went to PTA meetings and took them on trips. He also tried to sue his wife for custody, but it was impossible to win because the courts were biased toward women. So he continued to battle his wife in court. She wouldn't give up her sons because she wanted child-care payments to live on. But she allowed Andrew to take care of them.

Throughout those years Andrew didn't consider marriage. "I didn't want to bring my sons into a new relationship in the formative years—I didn't even think of it," he says. "I never had any problems in the area of female relationships, but some bright black women wanted more money than I had, and they didn't want to spend time with my sons.

"Some had standards that were too high in the

wrong area. They had an image of Prince Charming who would drive a Jaguar and take them to Tahiti on vacation. And I would say, 'Hey, look, I have a job and two kids, and I'm broke. But I can cook and keep house and give good talk. How about giving me a shot?' "

When Andrew was forty-seven and his sons were in college he met Nancy. "She was straightforward and she accepted me without reservations—as I was," says Andrew. "I liked the way she walked and how she carried herself. She picked up on my sense of humor, and that made me feel comfortable. She understood what I was saying. But I didn't think about marriage when we met. We became friends, and I discovered she was an honest person inside, not slick, and naive about a lot of things. She didn't challenge me or play games. She gave from the heart and she received, because she wasn't looking for anything in return."

When they married, Andrew insisted on a large wedding, and he wanted Nancy to wear a traditional white dress. "Women all want to be married and walk down the aisle—that's the day that is their day—that and having a child," he says. "Since Nancy's child-bearing years are gone, for me to deny her first dream would be wrong. She had to wait forty-three years for it, but I wanted her to have it. I love her, so why not?

"If you're not married, there's always a piece of you that can walk—that isn't committed. I didn't want that to happen. I've lived with women—I've lived without them—it's better with them. There are going to be ups and downs whether you're with someone or without someone, but when you're with someone and you're down, there's someone to lift you up and give you support."

Men Who Woo and Walk

Many men who seem to be caught up in a quest for the perfect mate are not simply driven by a desire for excitement. Their pattern of wooing and walking is often activated by anxieties about dependency that surface when they begin to feel connected to a woman. If they repeat this pattern of abandonment often, it may either stimulate or reinforce feelings that they are unworthy, because they are proving over and over again that they are failures. Eventually this cycle wears down their self-esteem, particularly if they value integrity in their work and in their other relationships. They wind up distrusting any woman who tries to love them, because they don't love themselves.

"A man gets you to the point where he's acceptable to you and you want to go ahead with it, and then all his insecurities kick in. You're disqualified because you want him," explained one divorced man who was single for fifteen years before he remarried. "If you really want him, how good can you be? He figures you'll probably end it when you find out what he's really like—so he might as well end it first to have control.

"On another level it's all about winning. Whether it goes back to Mommy, or problems in past relationships, or problems with self-esteem, he's got to win. He wants to get you committed—and as soon as you're committed, you've lost. He walks out and does it all over again."

Therapists say that men who repeatedly engage in this dance are often wrestling with a deep rage, their response to controlling parents, angry ex-wives, imperious bosses, and the world in general. When a woman becomes close to a man caught up in these conflicts, she may trigger these fears, and they become so overwhelming that a man can deal with them only by retreating. On a conscious level he may not like what he is doing because he knows that he is behaving in a hurtful and contemptible way, but he cannot control his unconscious need to flee.

According to Herb Goldberg, men who are the "most defensive, closed off, controlling, successfully manipulative and self-protective" are men who had "smothering, guilt-inducing, unconsciously hostile and manipulative mothers." As a response to this childhood experience, they develop a "compulsion to prove their manliness and release their anger by seducing and controlling women."[4]

Some men never resolve these conflicts because it's too difficult or painful for them to change. It's easier to continue the pattern and develop limited relationships in which they can maintain a distance. Other men manage to resolve these conflicts. This often occurs when the primary source of their anxieties—a controlling mother, for example, or a controlling ex-wife—recedes. Still others resolve the conflicts through therapy or by achieving mastery in their work or by developing sound relationships with other people.

"In the Midlife Transition a man can partially free himself from these images and anxieties," writes Daniel Levinson. "He is then less afraid of a woman's power to withhold, devour, and seduce. He can give more of himself, receive more from her, and accept her greater independence. He is more ready to work collaboratively with a woman or to work as a subordinate under her without feeling emasculated."[5]

"What Kind of Fool Am I?"

"I used to spend all my time running away from
women instead of running toward them. I was really
running away from myself," says Peter Paskin, a forty-
eight-year-old criminal lawyer in Washington, D.C. "I
wasn't comfortable with myself, so I wouldn't let a
woman see who I was or any of my inadequacies. I
thought I had to get through all my problems on my
own and show a front."

Peter, a tall man with a warm personality and a
quick mind who easily attracts women, attributes
many of his conflicts to his family upbringing. "My
mother was a powerful, selfish woman who painted a
picture that my father was not as successful as she
wanted him to be," he recalls. "I had one sister, but
I was my mother's favorite child, and I was given the
role of her champion—a role I resented because I
didn't want to compete with my father, whom I loved."

After graduating from Cornell Law School, Peter
married a woman who had been born in Iran. She
was beautiful, but after the birth of their daughter,
she developed serious emotional problems. They both
went to therapists and divorced when he was thirty-
two.

After they split up, his wife emotionally abused his
daughter and periodically threw her out of the house,
often as a retaliatory action against Peter. So Peter
maintained close ties with his daughter. He called her
every day and saw her every weekend. His anger toward his wife and his close bonds with his daughter
made it difficult for him to relate to other women.

Although Peter dated, it was impossible for him to
sustain relationships. He would pursue a woman dili-

gently for five months. Then, when the fear of real intimacy became overwhelming, he would stop seeing her. "Because of my deep ties to my mother, I was always drawn to powerful, attractive women," he says. "But I was afraid of being engulfed by their power because my mother engulfed my father—she was always putting him down. I could control my fear for a certain amount of time. Beyond that period of time I couldn't control it.

"Some women would complain that I wasn't receptive—that I was cold, arrogant, and closed. But when I liked someone, I would pursue her and see her every weekend and even during the week. Then I would suddenly cut her off. I was always convinced there was something wrong with her. One wasn't sophisticated enough; one wasn't the right religion; one had problems at work. And I would typically end relationships by not calling. I felt that by not calling I would hurt a woman less, and, besides, I didn't have the courage to say, 'You're not for me.' In retrospect I could have married almost any of the women I dated. The problem was always me—not them—but I denied this for a long, long time."

After years of repeating this pattern, Peter encountered a woman he had dated eight years before. Sharon was a brilliant lawyer and a striking brunette, twelve years younger than Peter. She also had deep bonds with her parents, which had blocked her from having ongoing relationships with men. When she first met Peter, she dropped him after four dates because she thought he was too old for her. But she really had too many fears of intimacy to see him.

When they met for the second time, Peter was forty-seven and Sharon was thirty-five. He asked her out and she accepted. They dated steadily for four months, and during that time Peter's mother became critically ill. His awareness that his mother was dying made him confront his own problems.

"I beat down on myself and said, Why can't I fall in love like other men? What's wrong with me? I felt cheated because I thought my mother was dying. I had devoted my primary emotions to her. How could she leave me? I thought if I could fall in love—and stay—it would ease the loss. Her impending death also brought me in touch with my own mortality."

Peter decided to reenter therapy to work on his conflicts and insisted that Sharon go with him. "Sharon had problems that I wanted her to resolve, and I had problems," he says. "She saw in me a strong, overpowering man, but when she was receptive to making a commitment, I became afraid. During therapy I felt the anger I had for women—and when I got in touch with it, it went away."

Seven months after they met, Sharon moved in with Peter. They married five months later. They're now planning to have a baby. "Sharon is a really good person, physically beautiful, and brilliant," Peter says. "Even though our fields of law are totally different, we have a lot in common—a high morality, a high regard for family, and we care about people. We have our problems—we fight a lot and disagree—but it's how you work out your problems that's important. Communication is the key. I became comfortable enough with Sharon to allow her to share my hopes and my fears.

"If you want to know what a man is all about, confront him—drag him to a therapist. Men can be honest to a point, but usually they don't know what makes themselves tick. They don't take the time to discover themselves and they spend time running away from the right women instead of toward them."

Men Who Love Too Much

We've all read a lot about women who "love too much." But women are not unique. Some men are drawn to women who aren't suitable as marriage partners for the same reasons that women are drawn to rejecting or undesirable men: They represent out-of-reach parental figures. Winning these women is tantamount to winning the approval of a critical mother or father. Obsession, after all, is not a uniquely female syndrome. Many of the classic stories about unrequited love, such as *Othello, Cyrano de Bergerac,* and *Of Human Bondage,* focus on powerful men who suffer profoundly because of their yearnings for rejecting women.

Nowadays men caught up in this syndrome are more guarded about revealing their feelings than women are. And because so many men keep their feelings to themselves, they may suffer even more profoundly than women when they become trapped in these patterns.

♦

"When my relationship with Meg broke up, I was a mess for three years because I was totally crazy about her and obsessed," says Gary Stewart, a forty-five-year-old divorced copywriter in Minneapolis, who has dark hair, a trim build, and an assertive manner. "I began questioning what was wrong with me and did the same kind of browbeating that a bachelor does. I couldn't seem to sustain a normal relationship with other women."

Gary married his college sweetheart when he was twenty-one. The marriage lasted fourteen years. "We didn't have children because my wife wasn't particularly maternal," he says. "She was career oriented, and I was uptight about that kind of responsibility. The marriage finally broke up because I was volatile and temperamental—a hard guy to live with—sarcastic, intolerant. Looking back, I wonder why my wife stayed with me as long as she did. Even so, it was a friendly breakup. We even went out occasionally after the divorce, as friends."

In his early thirties Gary met a married woman on a business trip. Meg was in her late forties and the mother of three children. Her marriage was in a shaky state. "I flipped over her," says Gary. "When I returned home, I began writing to her and calling. I couldn't get her out of my mind."

When he was thirty-five and his marriage ended, he dated several women and had a few relationships that lasted a year or more, but he continued to see Meg from time to time. Finally he persuaded her to go to Mexico with him. When they returned, he begged her to leave her husband and move in with him. "She had tremendous ambivalence because she had children and was Catholic," he says. "When her sons went off to college, she finally agreed, and we lived together for three years. I was forty and she was fifty-five. I was deeply in love with her and wanted to marry her and wasn't hung up on her age. She was incredibly attractive to me, and we had terrific sex."

Meg finally left Gary to return to her husband and family. When she did, he couldn't stop thinking about her. "To a great degree the obsession was sexual," he admits. "But I couldn't forget her or get her out of my mind. I couldn't get into any serious relationships. I met terrific women, but would seldom date them more than three times. I would ask Meg to join me on vacations, and she wouldn't. I would clip things in newspapers and send them to her. I'd do anything I could to maintain a tie."

His obsession lasted three years. "I began to doubt my ability ever to be in a sustained relationship with any other woman," he says. "I also knew I couldn't continue to be hung up on a relationship that would never materialize. I finally came to grips with it. I got angry at myself and said I had to stop. I ended all communication with Meg and psychologically moved her out of my mind because I really wanted to be married."

After pushing Meg aside, Gary decided to answer some Personals ads. "It seemed a valid way to meet someone," he says. "I ruled out ads that required a photo because that seemed like a meat market to me, or those that had religious criteria, or specific age criteria, because that also seemed narrow-minded. When I saw Judy's ad, it jumped out at me because she also worked in advertising. I figured we would have a lot in common. It was also extremely well written, head and shoulders above the others."

Judy was three years older than Gary, sweet and slender with bobbed hair and an ingenuous smile. They had a drink and dinner. They married five months later.

"On an early date I told her I doubted whether I'd ever get married again," says Gary. "Less than six months later we were married. We had the same basic values and mind-set on religion, politics, human relationships, friendships, and elderly people. She came across very quickly as gentle and shy. I was attracted to that.

"We said right away we were clones of each other. We don't have to run around all the time. We enjoy weekends in the country where basically we're not doing anything. Many people can't effect that balance.

They have to be in motion all the time. We just enjoy being together."

Bachelors in Their Prime

Divorced men are usually considered more viable as marriage partners than men who have never married at all, and for many of the same reasons that divorced women are often considered more marriageable than single women: They have fewer fears of bonding and are used to a married way of life. Yet once a man has been divorced for a long period of time, he is statistically just as likely—or unlikely—to marry as a bachelor who is his peer. Even so, bachelors, like single women, have to contend with stigmas that don't plague divorced men. They are considered either mama's boys, playboys, homosexuals, or just plain boys who can't seem to handle the responsibilities of marriage.

When I was in my late twenties, I became infatuated with a thirty-six-year-old lawyer and aspiring politician. We dated for a summer, and there was a very strong attraction on both sides. Then I learned the terrible truth: Jonathan lived at home with his mother. So did his younger brother, also a lawyer. They were both brilliant, outstanding athletes, handsome, and highly moral—so moral, they couldn't bring themselves to abandon their widowed mother. When I met her, I found out why. She was a powerful, magnanimous, and charismatic woman who had a strong hold on her two sons, neither of whom she consciously intended to keep at home.

Eventually Jonathan's brother moved to Florida, where he married a young woman and had a family.

Jonathan stayed home to mind the fort. When he was in his late forties, his mother died. Shortly afterward he met an energetic young lawyer who was determined to marry him. She finally did.

Of course not all bachelors live with their mothers, but often when a man remains single for many years, he has strong ties to his mother that prevent him from marrying. Other bachelors may have—and outgrow —the same kinds of conflicts that impede single women from marrying, or they may go through a generative crisis in midlife that spurs them to find a mate. "Some men cannot integrate their ties to their mother with ties to a wife and that is why they often do not marry until their mother dies," says Dr. Shaffer. "But if a man is not particularly neurotic, he can benefit from positive life experiences with the opposite sex and marry. Some of it is also luck—he has to meet the right woman who is either sufficiently different—or similar—to his mother."

During my early thirties I used to socialize with a group of men whom my women friends all wrote off as dyed-in-the-wool bachelors: They were bright, successful, attractive, and they were neither womanizers nor gay nor virgins. They were strictly heterosexual. Some of these men are still single. They will probably always be single. Others began marrying in their mid-forties. Some are now proud fathers, and when I asked why it took them so long to marry, they weren't even sure. They had been wanting to do it for years.

"My Defenses Were Down"

"I decided in my mid-thirties that I wanted to get married, but nothing seemed to work out," says Richard Morton, who married for the first time when he was fifty. "By the time I reached fifty, I was convinced that I was immune to the institution. If anything contributed to my not getting married, it was my conviction that I would not marry and could not marry."

Richard, a pleasant-looking trim man with a balding head and a mustache, grew up in an unhappy family; his parents were always quarreling and fighting. "I had an inordinate fear of marrying," he recalls. "I grew up in a home where my parents seemed to be people who tortured each other. When my friends married, I was surprised to find out they were relatively happy. Eventually I developed a more balanced perspective, but emotionally I still had trouble with the concept, even though I had some happy relationships that developed my sense of confidence."

Richard became a successful engineer. When he turned thirty-five, he decided to look for a wife. He began spending summers at a beach resort on the tip of Long Island where a lot of single people congregated.

"I was not a real swinger," he says, "but meeting women there was like shooting fish in a barrel. The problem was meeting a fish you really wanted. Even though I'd decided to marry, I still couldn't. I can't even say why. Consciously I thought I was available, but I wasn't. And the older I got, the more I met women who were my mirror images. They said they wanted to get married and would get heated about it, but when push came to shove, they got frightened."

In his late thirties, Richard began intensive psychoanalysis. He stayed with the process for eight years. "I felt desperate when I entered," he admits. "I wasn't happy with my work and I didn't have enough social contacts. I hoped analysis would either change my work or my relationships with women, because I realized I was going to lead a lonely life. It helped, but it didn't solve all my problems."

During the last four years of his treatment he prepared for a career change and entered law school in the evenings. He was forty-six when he graduated, and he got a job with a major law firm. He also terminated his analysis and bought a summer home, to which he invited friends.

He was still marriage-minded, but none of his relationships worked out. One lasted two years and then ended because he and his girlfriend weren't compatible on a day-to-day basis. Several others ended after a brief time because the women weren't available. "I wasn't threatening to marry them," he says, "but I was looking for a stable relationship. They may have sensed that I was in the marrying mode, and they broke off when it started getting more serious."

Toward the end of the summer he turned fifty, he met Roberta, a strong-minded psychologist with reddish hair and a nice smile. She was thirty-nine and had never been married. It was her first summer at the beach resort.

"I realized when I saw her that I could probably marry a girl like that—I liked her smile," he says. "But I'd had experiences like that hundreds of times. I was always meeting nice women I could marry. I didn't marry the others, so I figured I'd either get too tense or she would get too tense, or something would happen."

Then he ran into her at a party and spent the evening talking with her. "I found myself getting interested in her and got pissed off because she thought of me as a friend and told me about all the marvelous guys she had met that summer."

They met again at another party, and he made a pass at her. After that they began dating. "But it wasn't my intent to marry—because I had never married," he says wryly. "And because I was so convinced I wouldn't marry, I continued seeing her. For some reason she avoided scaring me off. Maybe it's because my defenses were down, and I was relaxed. She was easy to be with. We could be alone and do nothing and be comfortable."

They continued dating through the fall, and Richard warned her that his relationships never went anywhere. He talked about breaking off at times, but it was just talk. "She wasn't interested in stopping, so I deferred it in my own mind," he says.

Around Christmas, Roberta brought up the subject of marriage. "It was at a point where I was sufficiently hooked, and I wasn't scared," he says. "I could see myself marrying her and didn't want to terminate the relationship. I even tried to assure her she wasn't wasting her time and that we should play it out."

They married the following September—thirteen months after they met. "Sometimes when things get a little rough, you think you should go back to what you had initially," he admits. "But as rough as things get, it's clear you're not alone. Marriage isn't a panacea, but I'm happier now. I'm not lonely anymore."

◆

The men who are the most marriageable are those who have worked through their conflicts about bonding and those who have never had conflicts in the first place. It may take some men many years to work through these issues or to explore their fantasies. Other men don't need—or want—any time at all.

When a man marries is not nearly so critical as how he treats you and how he treats himself. It's possible to marry a man who is unreliable, depressed, unhappy, and unable to fend for himself. Is it desirable?

Men who have a healthy regard for themselves are more likely to be good partners than men who don't value themselves. Men who genuinely like women are more likely to be better as partners than men who are still angry at their mothers or ex-wives. Men who are happy in their work are easier to live with than men who are not.

All the men I interviewed said their mind-set was critical: When they were ready to marry, either they found the right woman or the right woman found them. Some men actively looked for a spouse. Others said they were receptive to the idea and didn't back off when a relationship became binding.

Yet it's usually not possible to find out a man's state of mind until you date him for several months. If a man *is* receptive to marrying you, he will try to develop closeness within a relationship instead of distance; he will try to create a feeling of security. If he is not available he will behave in ways that will make you feel insecure, anxious, and unloved.

"You never know how cold the water is until you stick your foot into it," advises Dr. Coopersmith. "You have to trust your gut feelings. Some men protest too much that they want to marry, yet they are really guarded and defended. Others may say they are hesitant about marrying, yet they wind up marrying. You have to give a man a chance and allow a relationship to grow before you decide."

ACKNOWLEDGMENTS

This book was inspired by the enthusiastic reception to my cover story for *New York*, "Brides at Last." I am indebted to my editor there, Deborah Harkins, for her commitment to the article.

While I was writing and researching this book, many people contributed their time, skills, and moral support. I am indebted to Connie Roosevelt, my editor at William Morrow, for her spirited guidance and for maintaining such high standards. Connie Clausen, my agent, was key in shaping the original concept and presenting it.

I am deeply grateful to Barbara Foley Wilson, a demographer at the National Center for Health Statistics, who generously made her files available. She spent many hours analyzing data for me and approving sections of this book that contain statistical material.

I am grateful to Lee Morgenlander and Sue Fried, survey research specialists, who helped me develop and evaluate the survey on dating patterns.

Many friends and colleagues read portions of this manuscript in various stages and made valuable suggestions. I am chiefly indebted to Shari Lewis, a devoted friend and superb editor, who read every word with care and offered invaluable editorial direction. I also wish to thank Guy Kettelhack, Gabrielle Propp, Rosyln Siegel, Marcia Schirazi, and Diane Finore, all of whom read portions of this book and gave me important comments. Thanks are also due to Patricia Rodimer, who helped me set up several key interviews; Myron Nadler, who provided assistance above and beyond the call of duty; Michael Pedalino, who helped provide research materials and lent important moral support; and all those friends who listened to me patiently and were there for me in critical times.

Finally I wish to thank my parents, May and Clifford, who have steadfastly supported my ambitions for many years and encouraged me to persist through dark moments; my sister Martha, for her unflagging support; and my brother, John, for his interest and good humor.

I cannot name the people who contributed their life stories, but I wish to thank all of them for being so generous and trusting in revealing intimate details of their experiences. I have tried to represent them as honestly as possible.

NOTES

PROLOGUE

1. The original findings were part of a report, "Marriage Patterns in the United States Today," by Neil G. Bennett and David E. Bloom, NB ER Working Paper #1701, September 1985. William Greer interviewed the authors and wrote an article about it that appeared in *The New York Times* on February 22, 1986.
2. *Newsweek*, June 2, 1986; *People*, March 31 and April 7, 1986; and *Wall Street Journal*, March 14, 1986.
3. See chapter 3 in Betty Friedan's *The Second Stage* (New York: Summit Books, 1981) for a fuller discussion of this view.
4. John Welwood, ed., *Challenge of the Heart: Love, Sex, and Intimacy in Changing Times* (Boston: Shambhala, 1985), p. ix.
5. Jane Gross, "Single Women: Coping with a Void," *The New York Times*, April 28, 1987.
6. Quoted in "Frustrated by the Odds, Single Women Over

Thirty Seek Answers in Therapy," by Elizabeth Mehren, *Los Angeles Times*, November 30, 1986.
7. Quoted in *ibid.*
8. Friedan, p. 87.

CHAPTER ONE

1. Jeanne E. Moorman, "The History and the Future of the Relationship Between Education and Marriage," unpublished report, United States Bureau of the Census, January 1987.
2. Larry Bumpass, James Sweet, and Teresa Castro, "Changing Patterns of Remarriage," Working Paper, Center of Demography and Ecology, University of Wisconsin, August 1988.
3. Peter Uhlenberg, Teresa Cooney, and Robert Boyd, "Divorce After Midlife," Working Paper, Department of Sociology, University of North Carolina, January 1989.
4. See "Marriage Study That Caused Furor Is Revised to Omit Impact of Career," *The New York Times*, November 11, 1989.
5. Demographic material in this chapter is derived from the National Center for Health Statistics unless otherwise cited.
6. *Advance Report of Final Marriage Statistics, 1986*, vol. 38. no 3, supplement 2 (Hyattsville, Md.: The National Center for Health Statistics, July 13, 1989).
7. Mrs. Wilson used the formula $q = 1 - e$ (e equals sum of the age-specific marriage rates) to develop her projections. She based her probabilities on two assumptions: (a) People would live at least until the age of sixty-five and thus there would be no competing risk of death in the calculations; and (b) the 1987 marriage rates would remain in force for that period of time. Her calculations differ slightly from those of Jeanne E. Moorman because she used marriage rates from 1987 and Moorman used rates from 1980 and 1985.
8. Arthur J. Norton, and Jeanne E. Moorman, "Current Trends in Marriage and Divorce Among American Women," *Journal of Marriage and the Family*, 49 (February 1987): 3–14.
9. *Population Series FM2*, No. 13, Table 1.1 (London: His Majesty's Service, 1981).
10. Robert Schoen and William Urton, Karen Woodrow, John Baj, "Marriage and Divorce in Twentieth-Century American Cohorts," *Demography* 22:1 (February 1985): 102–105.
11. See Marcia Guttentag and Paul Secord, *Too Many Women?*

The Sex Ratio Question (Beverly Hills: Sage Publications, 1983). The following discussion of the Middle Ages is also derived from this book.

12. *Ibid.*, p. 167.
13. Quoted in *ibid.*, p. 61.
14. See Bernice Rosenthal, "Love on the Tractor: Women in the Russian Revolution and After," *Becoming Visible: Women in European History* (Boston: Houghton Mifflin, 1977).
15. Beth Bailey, *From Front Porch to Back Seat* (Baltimore: Johns Hopkins Press, 1988), p. 35.
16. Quoted in *ibid.*, p. 37.
17. Quoted in *ibid.*, p. 38.
18. *Ibid.*, pp. 114–15.
19. Guttentag and Secord, p. 162.
20. Cowan and Kinder, *Smart Women: Foolish Choices* (New York: Crown, 1985).
21. Tracy Cabot, *How to Make a Man Fall in Love with You* (New York: Dell, 1987), p. 17.
22. *Cosmopolitan* magazine, August 1989.
23. Janice S. Lieberman, Ph.D., "Issues in the Psychoanalytic Treatment of Single Females Over Thirty," *Psychoanalytic Review*, in press.

CHAPTER TWO

1. Claudia Bowe, "What Are Men Like Today?" *Cosmopolitan*, May 1986.
2. Bruce Feirstein, *Nice Guys Sleep Alone: Dating in the Difficult Eighties* (New York: Dell, 1986), p. 21.
3. Heather Remoff, *Sexual Choice: A Woman's Decision* (New York: E. P. Dutton & Co., 1984), p. 14.
4. Timothy Perper, *Sex Signals: The Biology of Love* (Philadelphia: ISI Press, 1985), pp. 198–99.
5. See Remoff, pp. 58 ff., for historical discussion.
6. *Time*, January 8, 1979.
7. Sarah Hrdy, *The Woman That Never Evolved* (Cambridge: Harvard University Press, 1981), pp. 96 ff.
8. Herb Goldberg, *The Inner Male* (New York: Signet Books, 1987), pp. 204–6.
9. Beth Bailey, *From Front Porch to Back Seat* (Baltimore: Johns Hopkins Press, 1988), p. 15.

10. *Ibid.*, pp. 20, 23.
11. Cheryl Merser, *Honorable Intentions: Manners of Courtship in the 1980s* (New York: Atheneum, 1983), pp. 39, 42.
12. Chris L. Kleinke, Frederick Meeker, and Richard Staneski, "Preference for Opening Lines," *Sex Roles* 15 (December 1986): 597.
13. Perper, chapter 4.
14. *Ibid.*, p. 88.
15. Remoff, pp. 146–47, 154.
16. Letitia Baldrige, *Letitia Baldrige's Complete Guide to the New Manners for the 1990's* (New York: Rawson Assoc., 1990).
17. Shelley Juran, "Sexual Behavior Among Gays, Straights, Females and Males," paper presented at the annual meeting of the Society for the Scientific Study of Sex in San Francisco, 1988.
18. Perper, p. 215.
19. Robert Schoen, "Marriage and Divorce in Twentieth-Century American Cohorts," *Demography* 22:1 (February 1985): 112–13.
20. Remoff, pp. 193–95.
21. Margaret Mead, *Male and Female* (New York: William Morrow & Co., 1949), p. 342.
22. John Welwood, ed., *Challenge of the Heart: Love, Sex, and Intimacy in Changing Times* (Boston: Shambhala, 1985), p. xiii.

CHAPTER THREE

1. These statistics were derived from "Age Difference Between Bride and Groom," Work Table 14 (Hyattsville, Md.: The National Center for Health Statistics, 1987).
2. *Ibid.*
3. Davor Jedlicka, "Sex Inequality, Aging, and Innovation in Preferential Mate Selection," *The Family Coordinator*, April 1978, p. 138.
4. Data from the National Center for Health Statistics.
5. Barbara Gordon, *Jennifer Fever: Older Men, Younger Women* (New York: Harper & Row, 1988), p. 218.
6. Cited in *ibid.*, p. 46. The original source is *Lysistrata* by Aristophanes.
7. Wendy H. Baldwin and Christine Winquist Nord, "Delayed Childbearing in the U.S.: Facts and Fictions," *Population Bul-*

letin, vol. 39, no. 4 (Washington, D.C.: Population Reference Bureau, November 1984), p. 15.

8. Philip Blumstein and Pepper Schwartz, *American Couples* (New York: William Morrow & Co., 1987), p. 52.

9. See *ibid.*, p. 26.

10. *Sixty-fourth Report: Births, Deaths and Marriages in England and Wales* (London: Registrar General, 1901).

11. *Advance Report of Final Natality Statistics, 1987*, vol. 38, no. 3 (Hyattsville, Md.: The National Center for Health Statistics, June 29, 1989).

12. Daniel J. Levinson, *The Seasons of a Man's Life* (New York: Ballantine Books, 1978), p. 210.

13. Gordon, p. 12.

14. Virginia Houston, *Loving a Younger Man: How Women Are Finding and Enjoying a Better Relationship* (Chicago: Contemporary Books, 1987), p. 41.

15. Jedlicka, p. 137.

16. Sarah Hardy, *The Woman That Never Evolved* (Cambridge: Harvard University Press, 1981), p. 47.

17. Levinson, p. 232.

18. Blumstein and Schwartz, p. 161.

19. Gordon, pp. 20–21.

CHAPTER FOUR

1. *Trends and Variations in First Births to Older Women, 1970–86*, Series 21, no. 47 (Hyattsville, Md.: The National Center for Health Statistics, June 1989).

2. *Ibid.*, p. 8.

3. Wendy H. Baldwin and Christine Winquist Nord, "Delayed Childbearing in the U.S.: Facts and Fictions," *Population Bulletin*, vol. 39, no. 4 (Washington, D.C.: Population Reference Bureau, November 1984), p. 4.

4. Data provided by the National Center for Health Statistics.

5. Erich Fromm, *The Art of Loving* (New York: Perennial Library, 1989), pp. 44–46.

6. Betty Friedan, *The Second Stage* (New York: Summit Books, 1981), p. 86.

7. Kathryn Schrotenboer-Cox and Joan Solomon Weiss, *Pregnancy Over 35* (New York: Ballantine Books, 1985), p. 140.

8. Fromm, p. 47.

9. Schrotenboer-Cox, p. 10.
10. Data from the National Institutes of Health.
11. Cited in Schrotenboer-Cox, p. 9.
12. "The Saddest Epidemic," *Time*, September 10, 1984.
13. Cited in "Mommy Oldest" by Jeanne Kasindorf, *New York*, July 17, 1989.
14. Baldwin, p. 18.
15. *Ibid.*, p. 16.
16. See Arlie Hochschild with Anne Machung, *The Second Shift: Working Parents and the Revolution at Home* (New York: Viking, 1989).
17. "The Mommy Track," *Business Week*, March 20, 1989.
18. Linda Gunsberg, "A Cold Look at Motherhood Over 40," *Lear's*, September-October 1988.
19. Cited in "Mommy Oldest."

CHAPTER FIVE

1. Cited in *The Cosmopolitan Report: The Changing Life Course of American Women* (New York: The Hearst Corporation, 1986), p. 324.
2. See Jeanne E. Moorman, "The History and Future of the Relationship Between Education and Marriage," unpublished report, United States Bureau of the Census, January 1987. According to her calculations a twenty-five-year-old college-educated single woman has roughly an 87 percent chance of marrying, and a twenty-five-year-old high school graduate has roughly a 75.5 percent chance; a thirty-five-year-old single college-educated woman and a thirty-five-year-old high school graduate have roughly a 35.5 percent chance; a forty-five-year-old single college-educated woman has roughly a 10 percent chance and a forty-five-year-old high school graduate has a 12.5 percent chance.
3. See Janice Lieberman's paper, "Issues in the Psychoanalytic Treatment of Single Females Over Thirty," for a full discussion of the historical/psychoanalytic view of single women. Freud's views on women can be found in his essay "Some Character Types Met with in Psychoanalytic Work," *Collected Works* (New York: Basic Books, 1959), IV.
4. See discussion of these theories by Daniel Levinson in *The Seasons of a Man's Life* (New York: Ballantine Books, 1978), pp. 254, 322–32. Also see Gail Sheehy's *Passages: Predictable*

Crises of Adult Life (New York: E. P. Dutton & Co., 1974), pp. 272 ff., for her discussion.

5. Sheehy, p. 280.
6. Margaret Hennig and Anne Jardin, *The Managerial Woman* (New York: Doubleday, 1977).
7. "A woman shows her own value to her sisters by choosing a successful and personable man. It is probably a part of the process of natural selection, operating at the very outset of the courting game, and a healthy egotism at that, if only the criteria involved in such judgments were not so ersatz and commercial, and so trivial," writes Germaine Greer in *The Female Eunuch* (New York: McGraw-Hill Book Co., 1971).
8. Erich Fromm, *The Art of Loving* (New York: Perennial Library, 1989), p. 47.
9. Stanton Peele with Archie Brodsky, *Love and Addiction* (New York: Signet Books, 1976). See especially pp. 1–19.
10. *Ibid.*, p. 249.
11. *Ibid.*, p. 240.

CHAPTER SIX

1. Quoted in "Life on Midwest Farms Is Reaping Loneliness," by Dirk Johnson, *The New York Times*, February 28, 1988.
2. See Liz Hecht, "Stalking the Personals," *New York Woman*, June 1989.
3. See "Lawsuit Faults Fees and Practices of Dating Service Operator," by John McQuiston, *The New York Times*, February 13, 1990.
4. Judy Klemesrud, "Margaret Mead Puts Single Life in Perspective," *The New York Times*, January 25, 1974.

CHAPTER SEVEN

1. *Advance Report of Final Divorce Statistics, 1986*, vol. 38, no. 3, supplement 2 (Hyattsville, Md.: The National Center for Health Statistics, July 13, 1989). All other demographic data in this chapter was furnished by NCHS, unless cited otherwise.
2. Larry Bumpass, James Sweet, and Teresa Castro, "Changing Patterns of Remarriage," Working Paper, Center of Demography and Ecology, University of Wisconsin, August 1988.
3. See Erich Fromm, *The Art of Loving* (New York: Perennial Library, 1989).

Notes

4. Philip Blumstein and Pepper Schwartz, *American Couples* (New York: William Morrow & Co., 1987), p. 56.
5. Elizabeth Grauerholz, "Balancing Power in Dating Relationships," *Sex Roles*, vol. 15, 1986), p. 564.
6. Stanton Peele with Archie Brodsky, *Love and Addiction* (New York: Signet Books, 1976), p. 82.
7. Cited in Bumpass report.

CHAPTER EIGHT

1. Herb Goldberg, *The Inner Male* (New York: Signet Books, 1987), p. 50.
2. *Ibid.*, p. 53.
3. Daniel Levinson, *The Seasons of a Man's Life* (New York: Ballantine Books, 1978), p. 205.
4. Goldberg, p. 11.
5. Levinson, pp. 236–37.

BIBLIOGRAPHY

BAILEY, BETH. *From Front Porch to Back Seat*. Baltimore: Johns Hopkins Press, 1988.

BALDRIDGE, LETITIA. *Letitia Baldridge's Guide to the New Manners for the 1990's*. New York: Rawson Associates, 1990.

BALDWIN, WENDY H., and CHRISTINE WINQUIST NORD. "Delayed Childbearing in the U.S.: Facts and Fictions." *Population Bulletin*, vol. 39, no. 4. Washington, D.C.: Population Reference Bureau, November 1984.

BARRINGER, FELICITY. "Marriage Study That Caused Furor Is Revised to Omit Impact of Career." *The New York Times*, November 11, 1989.

BENNETT, NEIL G., and DAVID E. BLOOM. "Marriage Patterns in the United States Today." NB ER Working Paper #1701, September 1985.

Bibliography

BLUMSTEIN, PHILIP, and PEPPER SCHWARTZ. *American Couples*. New York: William Morrow & Co., 1987.

BOWE, CLAUDIA. "What Are Men Like Today?" *Cosmopolitan*, May 1986.

BUMPASS, LARRY, JAMES SWEET, and TERESA CASTRO. "Changing Patterns of Remarriage." Working Paper, Center of Demography and Ecology, University of Wisconsin, August 1988.

CABOT, TRACY. *How To Make A Man Fall in Love With You*. New York: Dell, 1987.

CARTER, HUGH, and PAUL C. GLICK. *Divorce: A Social and Economic Study*. Cambridge, Mass.: Harvard University Press, 1976.

CHERLIN, ANDREW J. *Marriage, Divorce and Remarriage*. Cambridge, Mass: Harvard University Press, 1981.

Cosmopolitan Report: The Changing Life Course of American Women. New York: The Hearst Corporation, 1986.

COWAN, CONNELL, and MELWYN KINDER. *Smart Women: Foolish Choices*, New York: Crown, 1985.

EHRLICH, ELIZABETH. "The Mommy Track." *Business Week*, March 20, 1989.

EXTER, THOMAS. "Your Chances of Marrying." *American Demographics*, July 1987.

FEIRSTEIN, BRUCE. *Nice Guys Sleep Alone: Dating in the Difficult Eighties*. New York: Dell, 1986.

FREUD, SIGMUND. "Some Character Types Met With in Psychoanalytic Work." *Collected Works*. New York: Basic Books, 1959.

FRIEDAN, BETTY. *The Second Stage*. New York: Summit Books, 1981.

FROMM, ERICH. *The Art of Loving*. New York: Perennial Library, 1989.

GOLDBERG, HERB. *The Inner Male*. New York: Signet Books, 1987.

GORDON, BARBARA. *Jennifer Fever: Older Men, Younger Women.* New York: Harper & Row, 1988.

GRAUERHOLZ, ELIZABETH. "Balancing Power in Dating Relationships." *Sex Roles,* Vol. 15, 1986.

GREER, GERMAINE. *The Female Eunuch.* New York: McGraw-Hill Book Co., 1971.

GREER, WILLIAM. "The Changing Marriage Market for Career Women." *The New York Times,* February 22, 1986.

GROSS, JANE. "Single Women: Coping With a Void." *The New York Times,* April 28, 1987.

GUNSBERG, LINDA. "A Cold Look at Motherhood Over 40." *Lear's,* September/October 1988.

GUTTENTAG, MARCIA, and PAUL SECORD. *Too Many Women? The Sex Ratio Question.* Beverly Hills, Calif.: Sage Publications, 1983.

HECHT, LIZ. "Stalking the Personals." *New York Woman,* June 1989.

HENNIG, MARGARET, and ANNE JARDIN. *The Managerial Woman.* New York: Doubleday, 1977.

HOCHSCHILD, ARLIE, with ANNE MACHUNG. *The Second Shift: Working Parents and the Revolution at Home.* New York: Viking, 1989.

HOUSTON, VICTORIA. *Loving a Younger Man: How Women Are Finding and Enjoying a Better Relationship.* Chicago: Contemporary Books, 1987.

HRDY, SARAH. *The Woman That Never Evolved.* Cambridge, Mass.: Harvard University Press, 1981.

JEDLICKA, DAVOR. "Sex Inequality, Aging and Innovation in Preferential Mate Selection." *The Family Coordinator,* April 1978.

JOHNSON, DIRK. "Life on Midwest Farms Is Reaping Loneliness." *The New York Times,* February 28, 1988.

JUNG, CARL G. *The Portable Jung.* New York: Viking Press, 1971.

JURAN, SHELLEY. "Sexual Behavior Among Gays, Straights, Females and Males." Paper presented at the annual meeting of the Sociey for the Scientific Study of Sex, San Francisco, 1988.

KASINDORF, JEANIE. "Mommy Oldest." *New York,* July 17, 1979.

KLEINKE, CHRIS. L., FREDERICK MEEKER, and RICHARD STANESKI. "Preference for Opening Lines." *Sex Roles* 15 (December 1986).

KLEMESRUD, JUDY. "Margaret Mead Puts Single Life in Perspective." *The New York Times,* January 25, 1974.

LEVINSON, DANIEL J. *The Seasons of a Man's Life.* New York: Ballantine Books, 1978.

LIEBERMAN, JANICE S. "Issues in the Psychoanalytic Treatment of Single Females Over Thirty." *Psychoanalytic Review,* in press.

LOVENHEIM, BARBARA. "Brides at Last." *New York,* August 3, 1987.

McQUISTON, JOHN. "Lawsuit Faults Fees and Practices of Dating Service Operator." *The New York Times,* February 13, 1990.

"Marriage Crunch, The." *Newsweek,* June 2, 1986.

MEAD, MARGARET. *Male and Female.* New York: William Morrow & Co., 1949.

MEHREN, ELIZABETH. "Frustrated by the Odds, Single Women Over 30 Seek Answers in Therapy." *Los Angeles Times,* November 30, 1986.

MERSER, CHERYL. *Honorable Intentions: Manners of Courtship in the 1980s.* New York: Atheneum, 1983.

MOORMAN, JEANNE E. "The History and the Future of the Relationship Between Education and Marriage." Unpublished report, United States Bureau of the Census, January 1987.

National Center for Health Statistics. *Advance Report of Final Divorce Statistics, 1986,* vol. 38, no. 2, supplement. Hyattsville, Md.: June 6, 1989.

———. *Advance Report of Final Marriage Statistics, 1986,* vol. 38, no. 3, supplement 2. Hyattsville, Md.: July 13, 1989.

————. *Advance Report of Final Natality Statistics, 1987*, vol. 38, no. 3. Hyattsville, Md.: June 29, 1989.

————. *Census of the Population Marital Characteristics*, PC 80-2 4C, vol. 2. Hyattsville, Md.: 1984.

————. *Married and Unmarried Couples, United States*, Series 23, no. 15. Hyattsville, Md.: 1982.

————. *Remarriage and Subsequent Divorces*, Series 21, no. 45. Hyattsville, Md.: January 1989.

————. *Trends and Variations in First Births to Older Women, 1970–86*, Series 21, no. 47. Hyattsville, Md.: June 1989.

————. *Trends in Postponed Childbearing, United States, 1970–87*. Hyattsville, Md.: 1989.

————. *Vital Statistics of the United States*, vol. II, Mortality Part A. Hyattsville, Md.: 1988.

————. *Vital Statistics of the United States*, vol. III, Marriage and Divorce. Hyattsville, Md.: 1984.

NORTON, ARTHUR J., and JEANNE E. MOORMAN. "Current Trends in Marriage and Divorce Among American Women." *Journal of Marriage and the Family*, 49:3–14 (February 1987).

NORWOOD, ROBIN. *Women Who Love Too Much*. New York: Pocket Books, 1985.

PEELE, STANTON, with ARCHIE BRODSKY. *Love and Addiction*. New York: Signet Books, 1976.

PERPER, TIMOTHY. *Sex Signals: The Biology of Love*. Philadelphia: ISI Press, 1985.

Population Series FM2, No. 13, Table 1.1. London: Her Majesty's Printing Service, 1981.

REMOFF, HEATHER. *Sexual Choice: A Woman's Decision*. New York: E. P. Dutton & Co., 1984.

ROSENTHAL, BERNICE. "Love on the Tractor: Women in the Russian Revolution and After." *Becoming Visible: Women in European History*. Boston: Houghton Mifflin, 1977.

Bibliography

"Saddest Epidemic, The." *Time,* September 10, 1984.

SCHOEN, ROBERT, WILLIAM URTON, KAREN WOODROW, and JOHN BAJ. "Marriage and Divorce in Twentieth-Century American Cohorts." *Demography,* 22:1 (February 1985).

SCHROTENBOER-COX, KATHRYN, and JOAN SOLOMON WEISS. *Pregnancy Over 35.* New York: Ballantine Books, 1985.

SHEEHY, GAIL. *Passages.* New York: E. P. Dutton & Co., 1974.

Sixty-fourth Report: Births, Deaths and Marriages in England and Wales. London: Registrar General, 1901.

UHLENBERG, PETER, TERESA COONEY, and ROBERT BOYD. "Divorce After Midlife." Department of Sociology, University of North Carolina, Chapel Hill, January 1989.

UNITED STATES BUREAU OF THE CENSUS. *Marital Status and Living Arrangements.* Current Population Reports, Series P-20, no. 433. Washington, D.C.: Government Printing Office, March 1988.

UNITED STATES BUREAU OF THE CENSUS. *Studies in Marriage and the Family.* Current Population Reports, Series P-23, no. 162. Washington, D.C.: Goverment Printing Office, June 1989.

WELWOOD, JOHN, editor. *Challenge of the Heart: Love, Sex and Intimacy in Changing Times.* Boston: Shambhala, 1985.

INDEX